D0387835

TRUST

Also by David Johnston

The Idea of Canada: Letters to a Nation

*Ingenious: How Canadian Innovators Made the World Smarter,
Smaller, Kinder, Safer, Healthier, Wealthier and Happier* (co-author)

BOOKS FOR YOUNG READERS

*Innovation Nation: How Canadian Innovators Made the World Smarter, Smaller,
Kinder, Safer, Healthier, Wealthier, Happier* (co-author)

TRUST

TWENTY WAYS TO BUILD

A BETTER COUNTRY

DAVID
JOHNSTON

SIGNAL

McCLELLAND
& STEWART

COPYRIGHT © 2018 DAVID JOHNSTON

Hardcover edition published 2018

All rights reserved. The use of any part of this publication reproduced, transmitted in any form or by any means, electronic, mechanical, photocopying, recording, or otherwise, or stored in a retrieval system, without the prior written consent of the publisher – or, in case of photocopying or other reprographic copying, a licence from the Canadian Copyright Licensing Agency – is an infringement of the copyright law.

Signal and colophon are registered trademarks.

Published simultaneously in the United States of America by McClelland & Stewart, a division of Penguin Random House Canada Limited, a Penguin Random House Company.

LIBRARY AND ARCHIVES CANADA CATALOGUING IN PUBLICATION

Johnston David, author
Trust / David Johnston
Issued in print and electronic formats.
ISBN 978-0-7710-4715-2 (hardcover).— 978-0-7710-4716-9 (EPUB)

Library of Congress Control Number is available upon request

Typeset in Caslon by M&S, Toronto
Printed and bound in Canada

Published by Signal,
an imprint of McClelland & Stewart,
a division of Penguin Random House Canada Limited,
a Penguin Random House Company
www.penguinrandomhouse.ca

1   2   3   4   5   22   21   20   19   18

*To children, who offer their trust instinctively
and with full expectation of fairness.*

Contents

Foreword

The Right Honourable Beverley McLachlin,
former chief justice of the Supreme Court of Canada

In this timely book, the Right Honourable David Johnston, Canada's twenty-eighth governor general, addresses one of the most important challenges of our day—how to maintain trust in ourselves and our institutions.

We live in a time when public confidence in individuals and institutions is under siege. Study after study reveals that Canadians trust their leaders, their institutions, and even one another less than they used to. And Canada is not alone. Trust in most democracies is decreasing. Yet without trust our democracies cannot function effectively.

This book identifies the causes of our world's declining levels of trust—the collapse of the post–World War Two consensus, reaction to economic inequality, and the digital age of instant communication that amplifies anger, stokes fear, and indulges pessimism. It then goes on to discuss how we can restore trust by making ourselves worthy of trust, by building trust around us, and by creating a more trustworthy and trusted country.

This book is no dry analytical work; rather, in the manner of a memoir, David Johnston tackles the subjects he discusses through the lens of his own rich experiences—as a boy growing up in rural Ontario, as a student and hockey player at Harvard University, as a law professor and university administrator, and finally as governor general of Canada.

The wisdom David Johnston has gleaned over a long life and a distinguished career shines through each short chapter. Whether taking on knotty questions of personal morality under the maxim "To thine own self be true" or offering practical advice like "Show up, not off," this book speaks to everyone who wants to be a better person and build a better country.

Along the way, it informs us. The book offers tantalizing insights into the education system, the justice system, and the responsibilities that come with the office of governor general—from meeting foreign dignitaries to overseeing the Order of Canada. And further, it tells stories that offer rare glimpses of the fascinating people David Johnston has met in his extraordinary life journey—people from whom he learned and whose wisdom he now shares with us.

We sometimes feel that our individual actions cannot make a meaningful and lasting difference in the complex world we inhabit. This book puts the lie to that feeling. It demonstrates that every one of us, high or humble, can work to increase trust in ourselves, our society, and our country.

Introduction

An invitation to trust

You have likely heard or read the popular expression about the importance of courage. Courage, the saying goes, is the first of human qualities because it is the one that guarantees all others. I am not convinced. I have a quality in mind that supersedes even courage in significance. Trust.

The *Oxford English Dictionary* defines trust as a firm belief in the reliability, truth, or ability of someone or something; or the acceptance of the truth of a statement without proof. While these definitions are technically accurate in capturing trust as a state of being and work in progress, these interpretations are far too modest in my eyes. Trust is bigger, more complex, and, ultimately, more important to us than any pedantic dictionary definition supplies.

Trust is the bedrock of democracy. Democracy—in Canada and in countries around the world—depends on a rule of law that strives toward justice. That rule of law depends on trust—a trust in each other as citizens, and a trust between citizens and the institutions that stand for and serve them.

Trust in these relationships means sharing a belief in basic facts. People who trust are reluctant to tailor facts to their views, instead of their views to the facts.

Trust in these relationships means knowing certain fundamental truths exist. People who trust are disinclined to trade in half-truths, myths, falsehoods, and conspiracy theories, even if these fictions serve individual interests.

Trust in these relationships does *not* mean those of us in democracies must agree upon absolutely everything, yet it *does* mean we must acknowledge the real state of the world—there is such a thing as truth; there are such things as facts; objective journalism is possible; history can be learned and learned from. If one does not consider anything to be true, if one believes facts are fungible commodities, if one thinks journalism is a sham and history a con, then the rule of law cannot work. And if the rule of law cannot work, then our democracy and its institutions are doomed.

These are the stakes. I raise them not merely to cause alarm, but so all Canadians can give trust the careful attention it demands. Strangely enough, trust is not something we spend much time contemplating. We tend to think little about trust because it is a curious quality that is almost always more noticeable in its absence than its presence—as something much more likely to be lost than gained.

This tendency is particularly pronounced among Canadians. We trust other drivers on the road to stop their vehicles when traffic lights turn red. We trust that individuals with similar incomes will get comparable treatment at tax time. And we trust the institutions and officials who represent and serve us to make decisions without favour to themselves and their friends. If we could not trust in these and countless other basic ways, our lives as individuals and our collective life as a country would be thrown into turmoil. As sociologist Niklas Luhmann wrote, "An absence of trust would prevent [us] from getting up in the morning."

While it is something that most of us take for granted, trust is a vital quality that grows stronger as it is acknowledged and then cultivated attentively. I think Hugh MacLennan's analogy of civilization as a garden and civilized people as gardeners comes the closest to capturing trust in our democratic way of life as the living, breathing result of careful thought and deliberate action. In *Voices in Time*, a novel that depicts a world in the wake of a nuclear holocaust, MacLennan writes:

> In the relatively rare periods in the past that we call civilized, people understood that a civilization is like a garden cultivated in a jungle. As flowers and vegetables grow from cultivated seeds, so do civilizations grow from carefully studied, diligently examined ideas and perceptions. In nature, if there are no gardeners, the weeds that need no cultivation take over the garden and destroy it.

To alter MacLennan's analogy slightly, trust is a flowering seed that must be cultivated, and we must be its diligent gardeners. Philosopher and ethicist Sissela Bok backs up this idea:

"Whatever matters to human beings," Dr. Bok wrote, "trust is the atmosphere in which it thrives."

4
—

Trust is not thriving in democracies today. According to Edelman—the global public relations company that has surveyed trust in countries around the world for two decades—trust in nearly all these countries is decreasing, dramatically so in some places. This lack of trust is a reflection and result of three interlocking trends.

First, our current lack of trust is a consequence of the collapse of the liberal democratic consensus in the West that stayed largely intact for some five decades following the end of the Second World War. This consensus—albeit one formed largely by and for white men—held that employers would supply decent pay, generous benefits, and healthy pensions to large swaths of the workforce. It further held that governments would create legal frameworks to regulate all manner of business and industry, address labour disputes, and limit the number and power of monopolies. And it also held that unions would play central roles in advancing gradually the overall welfare of not only workers but also marginalized groups such as women and people of colour.

Second, our current lack of trust is a reaction to the income stagnation and economic inequalities brought on by globalization in trade and commerce, technological disruption that has eliminated many traditional jobs and created a new super-wealthy elite, and the seeming helplessness—or, in some cases, apparent unwillingness—of democratic governments and other public institutions to redress these inequalities.

And third, our current lack of trust is a product of the digital age that has made information limitless, and communication not merely instantaneous but also constant. This age was meant to connect and enlighten us. And it has. Yet it has also amplified our anger, stoked our fears, and indulged our pessimism, which often override the connectedness and enlightenment, and which mischief-makers have encouraged to undermine our trust in our public institutions and each other.

This lack of trust globally troubles me, and the unstable state of trust in Canada gives me acute concern. I have spent much of my adult life contemplating trust. I started as a young law professor who was serving part-time as the very green research counsel to the Ontario Securities Commission, responsible for crafting new securities regulations for the province. Our three main goals in developing the rules were to reinforce confidence in the efficiency and integrity of the nation's capital markets; enhance the likelihood that credit would be used prudently and would increase prosperity; and, ultimately, assure Ontarians their deposits, savings, and pensions were secure and the trading of securities was honest and transparent—a fair deal.

I realized through this work that the proper functioning of capital markets depended ultimately on the trust of depositors and investors, and that the duty of the provincial regulator was to create and maintain rules and associated conditions necessary for that trust. My understanding of trust grew over the years, as I became more aware of its application and value beyond the laws of finance and into private enterprises and public institutions, communities and countries, and, most fundamentally, among individuals.

6
—

So what should we do to stabilize and revive trust? While we cannot restore the post-war consensus, erase all the imperfections of globalization, and shut down the Web, we can take meaningful action. We must first acknowledge that genuine trust is a kind of faith not leaped into blindly. Trust is gained through our actions and decisions, on our doing and not merely saying, on the basis of evidence that can be observed and measured rationally. As philosopher Onora O'Neill said during the 2002 edition of the BBC Reith Lectures, "Well-placed trust grows out of active inquiry rather than blind acceptance." Equipped with this understanding, we can then—with eyes wide open—identify, explore, and evaluate the attitudes, habits, and approaches that make a person trustworthy, that make a business, organization, or public institution trustworthy, and that make a country trustworthy. If we then start thinking and acting in the most effective ways—as individuals and professionals, as leaders and aspiring leaders, as representatives of businesses and organizations and officials of public institutions—we can restore and increase trust in our lives and in the life of our country.

This book is born out of a spirit of active inquiry and, equally important, practical application. I come at trust as a husband, father, and grandfather; as a lawyer, teacher, and university executive; and as a public servant who has chaired inquiries, led commissions, and, most recently, held the position of governor general of Canada. My seventy-seven years of life and my seven years as the representative in this country of Canada's head of state has enabled me to examine trust and then gain and apply some practical knowledge on how to be more worthy of trust as an individual; how to make the organizations and institutions I lead more worthy of trust; and how to develop a keener eye in spotting others who are worthy of trust.

In the pages that follow, I identify and explore twenty reliable ways each of us can take to repair, restore, and increase trust. The twenty are divided roughly into thirds—going from "me to we." The first third stresses the personal attitudes, approaches, and habits that make a person trustworthy. The second third concentrates on the actions people can take to strengthen trust in the communities in which they live and the businesses and organizations in which they work. I believe leaders and aspiring leaders of communities, businesses, and organizations will find many of these ways especially valuable as they carry out their roles. The final third explains and explores several ways of thinking and acting that whole democracies can carry out to become trusted not only by their citizens but also by other nations and their citizens. By democracies I mean not only the institutions and officials that constitute democratic governments but also the people who are represented and served by these institutions and officials—you and me.

These twenty ways are by no means the final word on trust. They represent my current thinking on this fundamental value, gained over more than seven decades and particularly refined during the seven years I served as governor general. They also represent a promise I made on my final day as governor general. For an editorial published in the *Globe and Mail* newspaper, I wrote that learning and trust were inseparable, and any society that is eager to learn and work together in an inclusive manner will see a sense of mistrust replaced by a sense of hope.

My hope is that you will reflect on the ideas and experiences recounted in these pages, adopt the ways of trust that work best for you, and apply them to build a better country—a more trusting and trusted Canada—for ourselves, coming generations, and the world.

Part 1

Make yourself worthy of trust

---

*Eight ways to think and act so that other
people view you as trustworthy*

I

Never manipulate

Trusting relationships depend on full, true, and plain disclosure,
and a commitment never to distort or deceive.

If I urge you never to manipulate, the onus is on me to come clean about why I am writing this book and what I expect from you after you have read it. My most pressing reason for writing this book is that I am on the last leg of my life's journey. If I do not write it now, I never will. My second reason is that I desire a better country. Without arrogance, I believe I have thoughts and experiences to share about how our country can be more cohesive socially, united politically, and prosperous economically—in short, a better country.

A most meaningful part of my experience is the privileged position I occupied from 2010 to 2017. Serving as governor general of this country was a cherished opportunity to see Canada from a special perspective—both by visiting communities across this land and by representing Canada in many countries around the world. This perspective enabled me to gain a clearer understanding of the many things we do right and some of the things that we need to improve.

From my tenure in that office stems my third reason for writing this book: having held that position, I believe I have an obligation to pass along to Canadians what I saw and learned from it. My main observation and lesson is that Canadians can make this good country an even better one by engendering more trust in each other, in the businesses and organizations of our country, and in the public institutions and officials that represent and serve us.

Which leads me to the next part of full disclosure: what I hope you will think and do as a consequence of reading this book. My hope is that you will gain a greater understanding of the role that trust plays in building a better country; I also hope the observations and advice I set forth in this book will help you become more worthy of trust yourself and give rise to more trustworthy organizations and institutions in Canada.

There is more. If you lead an organization, I hope you will think and act in ways that engender greater trust in your organization. If you do not lead an organization, I hope you will understand the thinking and actions organizations should take to encourage these organizations to think and act in trustworthy ways. Being more worthy of trust—as a person and an organization—is somewhat separate from (though not contradictory with) being more virtuous. It is a practical and essential element of creating a better country. That is what I am after. I hope I have made myself clear.

My first conscious exposure to manipulation and its connection to trust took place more than a half century ago. I was starting out in my career and had a minor part in crafting new securities regulations for Ontario. Truth be told, I was a very junior member of the team—a twenty-four-year-old assistant law professor at Queen's University who was hired pretty much to carry Purdy Crawford's briefcase for one summer. Purdy, who was on his way to becoming a legendary corporate lawyer, served as co-counsel of the committee that was reforming the law.

Through that experience, I recognized that when dealing with something as complicated and intangible as stocks and bond certificates that represent wealth, there are many opportunities for people to manipulate others, and that the manipulation could be murky enough to defy detection. This understanding led me to two conclusions. First, capital markets and our credit-based economy are essentially a web of trust relationships among owners, investors, employees, regulators, and, ultimately, citizens. When manipulation enters into this system by anyone at any point, trust erodes and the entire system starts to falter. Second, I concluded the most important step a jurisdiction such as the province of Ontario could take is to make sure the markets that rely on other people's money are as open as possible, and that the critical information within these markets be as accessible to people as possible.

After a while, Henry Langford, who was chair of the Ontario Securities Commission, thought it would be a good idea to have a position of part-time research counsel in the organization. I was put in this role and it gave me an opportunity to really dig into this subject. In time, I was named a part-time commissioner of the Ontario Securities Commission. Early on, I realized that the tangled web of deceit in domestic securities was so complex that it had an international component and that Canada therefore needed a federal presence in the regulation of securities markets and not merely provincial ones.

So one of the first steps we took as a provincial body was to prepare a report that recommended the creation of another body—the Canada Securities Commission. This institution would ensure that the Government of Canada participated in the regulation of markets, along with the country's provinces, both domestically and internationally. (While our recommendation was not followed at the time, I have faith it will be one day.) To prepare this report and inform many subsequent actions of the commission, we relied on the thinking of Louis D. Brandeis. The legendary United States Supreme Court justice wrote the national securities laws in his country that came into force during the early years of the Great Depression. He also wrote *Other People's Money and How the Bankers Use It*. Published in 1914, the book describes the combination of greed, lack of accountability, and poor oversight that plagued his country's securities markets at the time. (Fast-forward almost a century and the same factors were at the heart of the 2008 financial crisis in the United States and globally.)

Brandeis used his book to ask a fundamental question about trust and the securities market: When you are responsible for other people's money, do you treat it as if it were your own? The best way to bring about this kind of trust relationship, which Ontario and Canadian laws would emulate, is a principle known as full, true, and plain disclosure. The rule is based on the understanding that you cannot have a governing agency review every proposal to raise money from the public and then determine which proposals are ethical and sound financially and which are not. It is impossible for any regulator to do that and it is unwise to try.

So what you rely on is putting as much relevant information as you can in the open marketplace so people can make fully informed decisions. I want to stress the word "relevant." The information made available to the public must be closely connected or appropriate to what is being done or considered. Rather than exclude information that harms their case, manipulators will often bury it within a mass of information unrelated to the matter at hand. Brandeis summed up the matter neatly: "Sunlight is said to be the best of disinfectants; electric light the most efficient policeman."

Democracy works the same way. Full and true disclosure of relevant information in all aspects of a democratic society gives citizens the capacity to filter truths from falsehoods. An informed citizenry is then in a position to influence the laws and policies of its elected officials and institutions. When that notion of full and true disclosure breaks down—when a society has a press that is not free or that is narrowed, for instance—then a vital essence of democracy is lacking. An uninformed citizen is a voter who can be manipulated into voting for some strange things, without even knowing that their vote is being exploited. What makes it possible for a dictator or totalitarian to come to power is that people lose the capacity to remain informed.

All of which leads to this question: Don't elected officials in even the healthiest democracies manipulate people all the time? My answer is that an important distinction must be made between manipulation and persuasion. The worst leaders manipulate by failing to disclose vital information or by disclosing only the information that supports their views, decisions, and actions. The best leaders persuade in great part by being open about their motives and goals—just as I did my best to do at the start of this chapter—by disclosing as much of the information as possible to which they have access, and by making a conscious commitment to avoid manipulation and deception. Just imagine how much more worthy of trust each of us would be and each of our businesses, organizations, and public institutions would be if we simply made a conscious commitment never to manipulate and never to deceive.

When I look back on my many years as a university executive, I could have been accused of being a manipulator if it were not for the vital fact that I tried my best to be open about my motives and goals, made relevant information available to others, and gave credit to others when things went right and took blame when things went wrong. Leaders can accomplish almost anything they want as long as they do not take all the credit. On the flip side, leaders can prevent the rapid erosion of trust by taking responsibility for wrongs, because assuming ownership of the problem removes the temptation of trying to manipulate your way out of the problem.

You would be surprised by how willing people are to move on to tackle a problem once a person in authority takes it upon himself or herself to shoulder the blame for the problem. My friend Dr. Richard Cruess provided a great example of this lesson some thirty years ago. An orthopaedic surgeon by training, Dr. Cruess was dean of medicine at McGill University during almost all my years as principal of the school. Along with being a superb university leader, he became my good and trusted friend.

One day, I was sitting in my office and the school's top communications person came in and said to me, "You'd better turn on the television. There is something going on at Royal Victoria Hospital that you should see." So I turned on the TV and there was Dr. Cruess standing before many reporters and cameras, explaining how the hospital had just discovered that one of its obstetricians had been performing surgical procedures even though he was HIV positive. Dr. Cruess explained that the final-year resident, who had rotated through several McGill University–affiliated hospitals, had not known he was HIV positive. When he became acutely ill, he informed authorities immediately and was then reassigned to nonclinical duties. Dr. Cruess went on to say that the resident had done nothing wrong, that he would not be performing any further surgical procedures, and that he had been granted a leave of absence to be treated for his illness.

When the news conference ended, I was concerned about damage to the university's reputation, so I phoned Dr. Cruess and said, "Dick, what the heck were you—the dean of medicine at McGill University—doing over at the Royal Victoria Hospital, which is responsible for its own clinical practice, shouldering

17
—

responsibility for this problem?" He replied very calmly, "Because nobody else was prepared to." I said, "Thank you, Dick. I appreciate your explanation."

And that was that. I realized that he acted as he did because he knew about the facts of that particular drama, because he knew that people looked to him as a leader, because he was capable of speaking about difficult subjects in a clear and direct manner, and above all else because he realized what the consequences would be for the hospital and for health care in the city if no one were willing to step forward and accept responsibility. Yes, McGill University had a training relationship with the hospital, but this problem had little to do with that relationship. Dr. Cruess took responsibility because he saw the urgent need for someone in authority to act in a way to preserve trust in the hospital, or at least prevent a substantial erosion of that trust. Other people at the hospital had more direct responsibility, but they were much less inclined to step forward. As a result of Dr. Cruess assuming ownership of the problem and not trying to manipulate out of the problem, the hospital could start remedying it and making amends for any harm done from a position of trust.

Dr. Cruess's example is a powerful lesson to us all. Disclose fully and truly. Share credit. Accept responsibility. And, above all, never manipulate and certainly never deceive. I hope I have made myself clear.

2

To thine own self be true

Getting a firm fix on your values is the surest
guide to trusting behaviour.

To thine own self be true,
And it must follow, as day the night,
Thou canst not then be false to any man.

These three lines from Act I, Scene 3 of William Shakespeare's
most celebrated play, *Hamlet*, are the fatherly advice spoken by
Polonius to his son Laertes as the young man leaves Denmark to
study in Germany. With them, Polonius raises some basic questions not only for his son to ponder, but also for us: How does
one separate truths from falsehoods? How does one choose what
qualities to value? How does one come to trust in their chosen

values and use them to chart a course in life? These are big, important questions for all people of every age.

I appreciate Shakespeare's brilliance more as I grow older. He had a way of capturing and expressing so many classic questions and dilemmas in life, and did so in such poetic phrases and passages. The Bard of Avon was a profound student of human nature who saw some universal qualities in us and explored them through the dominant medium of his day. As we come to learn in the play, the advice offered by Polonius is more urgently needed by the Prince of Denmark. Hamlet is a fellow who does not seem to have a clear set of values, and this lack leaves him thrashing about—physically and emotionally—in a state of confusion and doubt. He cannot decide how he should respond to the murder of his father, the king, because he has no firm principles by which to govern his decisions and guide his actions.

I am not saying Hamlet's dilemma is an easy one to resolve. After all, how many of us have been visited by the ghost of our father? Yet, when I was about Hamlet's age, I faced an eventful decision of my own. At the start of my sophomore year at Harvard College, way back in 1960, before the U.S. civil rights movements gained worldwide prominence, I had just joined one of the school's prestigious clubs for undergraduates, known as final clubs. Shortly thereafter, a fellow student from Nigeria was under consideration for membership. He was rejected. Members of the selection committee said they made their decision to deny the Nigerian student because they believed club alumni, who supported the club financially, were not ready to have as a member a man whose skin is black in colour. There were only a few black students at Harvard at the time. When I learned about the committee's decision, I resigned from the club. My decision was not made to make a public stand against injustice or to right a wrong. I was not trying to be a saint, and I did not want to be any kind of martyr. I was simply uncomfortable being a member of a club that had just denied membership to a man based solely on the colour of his skin. I believed in equality, humility, and empathy, so the club's decision rubbed me the wrong way.

Again, my decision to resign was not meant to be a public stand against racism. I was most concerned about getting good grades and playing good hockey. I would have preferred if everyone had forgotten about the whole thing completely. While this matter hit my particular set of values in a way that made my decision uncomplicated and clear, I did not at the time view my decision through the lens of "to thine own self be true." I did not have the self-awareness at age eighteen that I could say to myself, "I have this set of values. At this time, they are different than the values of other club members; so I will go a different way. There will be some consequences to my decision; yet so be it." My thinking was not that sharp or self-aware. I just had a strong sense of discomfort at the whole situation, and it was this discomfort that made my decision a simple one. When I had sincere discussions with friends, who told me I was making a mistake and that the whole situation would work itself out in the end if I would just go with the flow, I did not tell them that my set of values were better than theirs. I just did not want to be part of an organization that has a membership principle of that kind. I usually capped my case by saying,

"Hey, I'm a kid from a little town in northern Ontario in Canada. It's not part of the mainstream of the United States, so I'm not trying to challenge the status quo in any way. I'm just trying to do what I think is right for me."

One of those friends was Michael Deland. Mike was a junior varsity hockey player at Harvard, as well as a member of another final club at the university. He later served for many years with the U.S. Environmental Protection Agency, as chairman of the president's Council on Environment Quality, and as chair of the U.S. Council on Disabilities. Mike came from an accomplished and distinguished family. His father was a lawyer and later served as chairman of the board at Harvard; his grandfather was a respected Harvard-trained judge. At the time I made my decision and this controversy broke out, I went to dinner one evening at Mike's parents' house. Theirs was a lovely country estate and his grandfather happened to be there. We did not discuss this club matter at the dinner table, but afterward I was walking in the garden and Mike's grandfather came over to me and put his arm around my shoulder. I had not met him before. He said: "Son, I understand from my grandson that you've been through a difficult decision and you've paid a bit of a price for it." I said: "Yes, Judge Deland. I guess I have." He said, "Well, I just want to say you did what you thought was right and that's the important thing." He did not say I was right. He said I did what I thought was right. That is a critical distinction, because it speaks to the idea at the very heart of the phrase "to thine own self be true"—follow the course you believe to be true for yourself.

Three years later, in my senior year, the situation had changed dramatically. Across the United States, the civil rights movement had become more visible and influential. This change was apparent even at Harvard. Many more African-American students were being admitted as undergraduates. In my case, I was elected one of four class marshals for my graduating class in 1963; another was an African-American student, who later became a distinguished lawyer in Washington, D.C. A class marshal is responsible for bringing everyone together for reunions and appointing other graduates as agents to raise money for the school on behalf of the graduating class. I was a bit surprised at my election, because I was not part of the 10 per cent elite from the fraternities and final clubs. I was enormously flattered and also aware in a small way that my decision three years earlier had now been accepted and was respected by my classmates. I would not have guessed three years earlier that I would be elected class marshal. My classmates' consideration of my action had gone from indifference or disagreement to a tangible expression of trust.

This decision and its consequences taught me a lesson in the value of getting a fix on my values and then trusting these moral instincts to guide my behaviour. Mine are equality of opportunity (I believe everyone has the right to reach for their full potential), humility (I am open-minded, aware of my limitations, and appreciate the wisdom of others), and empathy (I am aware of the situations and feelings of others). I have found since that most personal decisions I have had to make over the years came easily because I had a clear sense of the kind of person I was—or at least wanted to be—and I placed my trust in that knowledge. I also came to learn that most people trusted me because my personal decisions were consistent and founded on something stronger than whims and circumstances.

All of which leads to an obvious question: How do you go about ensuring you are exposed to the influences necessary for you to cultivate the values you need to inform your decisions? During my installation speech as governor general, I said that if you were to remember only three words from my remarks, make them "Cherish our teachers." I went on to say that if we had a whole day together I would tell the stories of one hundred teachers, mentors, coaches, and community leaders who have instilled in me the values by which I have made a lifetime's worth of decisions. I have been lucky in that respect. I also realize that teachers of all kinds exist outside classrooms. They are all around us, and the trick becomes which of them to identify, study, and emulate. Canada's honours system is a great vehicle by which to do the trick. My advice to any young person in our country is to look to the people Canada has honoured. There you will find your role models and, from them, some clear cues about the kinds of values by which you should live.

One of the main reasons I helped set up the Rideau Hall Foundation while I served as governor general is to amplify more clearly and loudly the names of the Canadians who are honoured so that more people, especially younger people, are aware of them. The Order of Canada is the most notable award in our honours system. With more than 3,500 members, officers, and companions, its motto is "They desire a better country." But it is just one of seventy different honours for which the office of the governor general is responsible. Over time, the foundation hopes to promote, through education, our country's honours system and, in doing so, the fundamental values that have made Canada a special country. The effort is the foundation's way of saying, "Let's all look to these people we honour to become aware of what values they hold that make them so special, and then let's adopt those values for our own lives." (I have much more to say, in a later chapter, about honouring this kind of teacher.)

The foundation's mission is why I believe strongly in the non-political nature of Canada's honours system—so much so that, even though the governor general is responsible for the process, I made a point while I served in the role that I would not personally involve myself in the granting or removal of any honours, other than signing into effect the recommendations of the advisory council. Even though the office I held was outside of politics, I did not want any perception of personal influence in even the slightest way to tarnish the honours system. It is that critical to the process of recognizing and thereby nurturing the values that we as Canadians wish to uphold. I crystallized this matter in a letter to the Chief Justice of the Supreme Court, who has chaired the advisory council since the Order of Canada's inception in 1967. It ended as follows:

> I would echo the principles agreed between my predecessor, the Right Honourable Roland Michener, and then Prime Minister, the Right Honourable Pierre Trudeau:

> *It is my view that the Advisory Council must appear to be, and be in fact, completely independent, as much from the Chancellor*

of the Order, on the one hand, as it is from the Government, on the other.

Above all, then, it is my intent to ensure that the principles of merit, impartiality and accountability are adhered to in all aspects of the management of the Order.

To further nurture the values we wish Canadians to uphold, the country put in place some new awards, including the Governor General's Innovation Awards, which we want to use to make the culture of innovation a standard feature of being Canadian. The awards for innovation are a way of encouraging Canadians to come into any job or task with a constructively critical attitude that asks, "How can we think about and work together to do this better?"

I am not saying that getting a fix on your values is easily done. This can be tricky terrain to tread. Some people view core values differently. So you have to be careful. I often think about the source of a person's values. Do these values—the beliefs that guide their decisions and actions—come from a place of respect, generosity, and kindness, or from some other place that is not so attractive? This is also one of the rare cases in which I emphasize the first-person singular rather than the first-person plural. I do so because I think the values that guide you have to have been processed over years of experience so they become a part of you, so they become your point of reference when you find yourself in difficult situations.

This process takes consideration and reflection. I encourage you to take that time to reflect. Find your values. Trust in their wisdom. Use them to guide you. To thine own self be true.

3

Listen first

Trust grows when you take time to understand the
thoughts and feelings of others before you act.

My grandmother told me that people were given two ears and just
one mouth for a good reason: we should listen before we speak. She
was a wise woman and an early proponent of what we refer to now
as emotional intelligence. While that term gets bandied about quite
a bit these days, emotional intelligence at its core is the simple act
of listening to and empathizing with another person—and using
that listening and empathizing to inform your decisions and actions.
At the risk of earning my grandmother's wrath, let me share with
you a few of my thoughts and experiences about her wise words.

My first thought centres on Sir William Osler. He is perhaps
the foremost proponent of listening first. He is certainly the

first person to exhibit this critical behaviour of which I became aware. Born in 1849 in a small town north of Toronto, Osler was in his day the most famous physician in the English-speaking world. Today, he remains one of the most influential figures in the history of medicine. His reputation stems in large part from his landmark book, *The Principles and Practice of Medicine*, which went through more than forty editions over a century. Fundamental to Osler's approach as diagnostician and teacher was to place himself and his students in the hospital wards and close to the bedsides of patients—even before reaching for their charts. Here, Osler and his students could listen carefully to what patients had to say about their conditions. (Osler and his students could also listen to what their patients' bodies— through palpation or examining by touch, and through auscultation or listening to sounds made by the heart, lungs, and other organs—had to say.)

Listening to patients serves two vital functions. First, the physician is gathering evidence on which to diagnose the patient's ailment, remedy that ailment, and heal—hopefully—the patient. Second, the simple act of listening fosters trust by the patient in the physician, making it more likely the patient will follow any instructions or recommendations from the physician about treatment or intervention. The trust that emerges from this physician-patient rapport serves them both. This method certainly sounds obvious to us today. Yet it was considered revolutionary in North America at the time. Until Osler came along, medical teaching was done through textbooks and in lecture halls, while the difficult practice of diagnosis was performed with scant input from patients. The hierarchy between teachers and students, and between doctors and patients was similar to that practised in the military. Officers (like physicians) kept a distance from their subordinates to maintain the discipline inherent in the relationship. Since then, generations of physicians at home and around the world have adopted Osler's principle of listening first. It has many benefits, the most important being the impact this approach has on the health of patients.

That is a very human and up-close-and-personal perspective. What benefits does genuinely listening first produce in organizations, especially public ones? A big benefit is that organizations get some good ideas to which they might not otherwise be exposed. Diversity is a creative force, and when an organization gathers a diverse group of people in a room or around a table, that organization is likely to get some ideas that can improve it. Another benefit of listening first is that these same people feel happier about their jobs, which makes for a more productive workplace. Most people want to go home after a long day and feel they have contributed to something important. They are much more likely to feel that way when they are listened to, as opposed to always doing the listening.

An organization's work is not done yet. After ideas have led to decision, action, and achievement, the organization should celebrate what has been accomplished and give credit where it is due. As a leader of the organization, you can accomplish so much more if you insist on never receiving credit for it. Even when an achievement stems from an idea that is mostly yours, you are wise to give credit generously to others.

Of course, listening cannot go on and on: you have to give fair consideration to what you hear (which means you do not always have to do exactly what people tell you) and then decide. At the same time, you cannot engage in empty listening: you cannot go through the motions of listening and at the end of the exercise toss aside every idea and act in your own way. While the first pitfall rarely occurs, the second is common and is a fatal flaw in listening first. If an organization sets up a system through which to listen and it does not act consistently with respect to what it is being told, then it has dashed expectations, diminished trust, and done more harm than good. People become jaded and cynical, believing the whole listening exercise has been a waste of time. And they would be right. I see this very situation when large organizations distribute questionnaires to gauge the opinions of employees and gather their ideas—and then leaders of these organizations make few if any meaningful moves as a consequence.

There also is a flip side. Those doing the talking have a responsibility to test their ideas with peers before advocating that the entire organization adopt their suggestions. Maybe there is a grave imperfection in their idea? Even if there is not a serious defect, there is likely room for improvement.

While organizations should be cultivating atmospheres in which other people's ideas are taken seriously, the people within the organizations should be cultivating places in which their ideas are offered seriously. We were able to strike that balance at Rideau Hall. Before I began my first day as governor general, I asked the Secretary to the Governor General to get me the current strategic plan for the institution. I wanted to read it. When I was told there was not one, I asked the Secretary to go into the organization's archives and find past strategic plans. I figured I was not the first new sheriff in town, so there must be earlier examples we could draw on for guidance and inspiration in answering some basic questions: What has this office always done? What does it want to do in the future? How will it go about doing that? And how does it measure its actions to reach its goals?

It turned out there was no document, or not one that could be found. So now what? It also turned out that the Secretary, who is the top public servant in the organization and who really runs the place, was retiring and we were carrying out interviews with the top applicants to find a replacement. So one of the main questions I put to each of the candidates was this: How would you go about developing a strategic plan for this organization?

The person who hit the ball out of the park with his answer was Stephen Wallace. At the second and final interview of remaining applicants, I asked each to prepare an outline that describes how to develop and implement such a plan. Again, Stephen nailed it. I asked him how long it would take to prepare a plan. He replied that he could do it over a weekend if that was what I wanted. But if we truly wanted the plan to work, he and the senior team should take three months to consult every part of the organization. So that is exactly what we did. We met with everyone, listened closely to them, and responded with a plan that reflected their ideas and pointed the organization in some new directions: we would take some bold steps to make the role and activities of the Office of the Governor General, as well as the offices of the provincial lieutenant governors and territorial commissioners, better known to the people of Canada; we would broaden the honours system and attempt to make it better known; we would establish communications systems internally so that the voices of all the members of the team would be heard (the strategic plan itself being the first example of this direction in action); and we would build mechanisms to enable the organization to adjust the plan and its directions as changes in our operating environment arose.

I must admit that some of the priorities in the plan were different from ones I would have proposed. But because they were high priorities of the people who made up the organization, Stephen made sure the plan reflected them. If we did not do so, the listening we did would have been rendered meaningless. People recognize that sort of insincerity pretty quickly, and their trust in the organization and its leaders erodes as a result. Again, if you are committed to a group exercise, the opinions and ideas of the group should be reflected in what you decide and act upon. That meant some ideas I would not have prioritized were made priorities. A good many turned out to be successes.

So I was wrong—happily so. Even more, I was overjoyed and enormously satisfied at the institution's performance that emerged out of the plan and pleased that the effort to create it built trust and cohesion among our team. The job of a leader, if he or she is truly listening, is not descending from the mountaintop and presenting his or her organization with commandments carved in stone. A leader also must listen to the people whom that leader needs to make the organization work.

Was I entirely satisfied with our performance all the time? No, of course not. Who is? That is only natural when you are trying to change an organization. Yet when we finished the seven years, our office was named top public-sector employer in the region. Stephen Wallace's leadership on several fronts, but especially in working with the whole team to develop and implement the strategic plan, was largely responsible for this success. And that plan was the result of listening to the people within our organization. Listening genuinely, and then acting on what we heard, had upped our performance as an organization.

Our success was evident in other ways. Each year, federal public servants are invited to fill out employee-satisfaction surveys. Our organization's response rate went from 60 per cent to 85 per cent, which I interpret as being a result of our organization's willingness and effort to promote a culture that stresses listening first. Employees in our organization became more willing, confident, and trusting to share their views through many avenues because they had become accustomed to having their views treated seriously and having them reflected in the organization's actions.

Another example of our success through listening was an independent review of our operations that was undertaken by Jim Mitchell, a retired senior public servant. The review was carried out at the point when my five-year tenure was extended by two years. Mitchell concluded that the people at Rideau Hall were the best group of public servants he had seen in his career in government in their professionalism, dedication, and the pride they take in their jobs. He also had a warning. He said these proud and dedicated people were working at their limit; he cautioned there was a tendency in our organization to add more things for people to do because our ambitions were so many and far-reaching. Do no more, he recommended, and if you are tempted to do more on one hand, do less on the other.

How did we respond to this recommendation? Like any good organization would: we listened.

4

Be consistent

Trust builds when you bring the same temperament and character to your public and your private behaviour.

Bank of England governor Mark Carney has a wonderfully vivid and perfectly truthful saying about trust: "Trust arrives on foot and leaves in a Ferrari." The earlier version of this maxim, from pre-automobile times, is: "Trust comes in on foot and leaves on horseback." It arrives on foot because it is slow to build, and it is slow to build because it is based on behaviour that is consistent and consistently positive over time. Rarely do we make a definitive judgement about someone's trustworthiness based on a single encounter or conversation. Nor should we expect others to trust at first glance. Trust is earned incrementally and granted with greater acquaintance. The same cannot be said for the loss of trust. It often speeds off at the first sign of doubt and usually at the first suggestion of deceit. Very often, that trickery makes it possible for us to see for the first time what has been going on behind the wonderful wizard's curtain all along. I do not see anything wrong with the unevenness of this equation. All good things come only through time and effort, do they not?

My experience has taught me that the best way to build up trust is to act consistently. The simplest definition of acting consistently is bringing the same temperament and characteristics to your actions whether you are in public or in private. I call that consistency running hard on the backstretch. It is not my phrase originally. I learned it as a teenager when I attended a summer leadership camp run by the provincial government at Bark Lake, which is along the Madawaska River in Ontario. The two camp directors were terrific guys, mentors whom I really cherished at the time and whom I have remembered all the years since. The whole group would gather for a fireside chat every evening. At one such chat, the directors talked about the importance of running hard when the crowd is not watching. When you are running around a track or, even better, cross-country, there are portions of the race when you are near the crowd and other stretches where there is no crowd, or the spectators are off in the distance. The questions you ask yourself in these instances are "How do I perform when people aren't watching me or aren't watching me closely? Do I run as hard going down the backstretch as I do when I'm going past the grandstand?" Grandstanding is the opposite of running hard on the backstretch. It is harder to function consistently in the backstretch because you do not have the adrenaline flowing in your veins the same way you do when you are running along in front of the grandstand where the fans are cheering you on. When you are alone, with only the track or the woods for company, you have to dig a little deeper.

Stepping out from my metaphor, the questions become "Do I act privately in ways that are consistent with how I act publicly? How do I behave when no one is watching or when I am dealing with a person one on one, as opposed to within a large group of people?" And keep in mind: in an organizational or business setting, private does not always mean being alone. It can mean being a leader together with a tight circle of advisors or board of directors. These situations can be considered private because the leader is confident his or her words and behaviour will remain behind closed doors.

So how do you make sure you act consistently in public and private, and through that steady behaviour make yourself worthy of trust? I have learned that you do so by thinking and taking action that is long term and big picture. A good example of long-term, big-picture thinking and acting comes from my years as an educator, especially meetings of the Dean's Council at the University of Waterloo. At the time, the council was made up of the six deans, two vice-presidents, the provost, and the president. I learned quickly that, to be effective and trusted, each member of the council must come to these gatherings not as a representative of a narrow interest, such as his or her faculty, but as a representative of the university as a whole—its students, professors, staff, alumni, and especially its long-term mission. You have to resist the temptation of using council meetings, and settings like them, to further narrow interests or secure particular advantages. You cannot enter the room thinking, "I'm dean of the faculty of science and at last I'm at the centre of power, so I'm going to secure for my faculty and its disciplines as much as I possibly can." If you adopt this attitude, your colleagues will listen to you politely at the first meeting. At the second, they will start to push back on your demands. And at the third, a senior dean will take you aside and quietly ask you to cut it out. No single faculty or department automatically merits more than another. "We all work hard," that person will likely hear. "We all believe our particular faculty is deserving of more resources. Start thinking of the greater good of the entire university, which means thinking long term and big picture."

That does not mean you should stop altogether being an ardent defender of your faculty and discipline, but you do need to start taking actions and making decisions that are in the best interest of the institution as a whole, especially when you are in a forum making judgements for the whole institution. If you are a leader who manages this conversation properly, you tend to appeal to and bring out the best qualities in people. They tend to start looking bigger picture and longer term. They tend to realize the trust that is being placed in them, and they no longer become merely the agent of an interest. They are the institution.

Adopting this kind of attitude has real benefits. For instance, when the president and provost say to the group, "We have a real problem on our hands. We have to cut our overall budget by 5 per cent. We can respond by whining about how the government is treating us. We can make an across-the-board cut so that everyone experiences the same fate. Or we can take the challenge as an occasion to ask ourselves who we are as an institution and then use that self-knowledge to identify the compelling priorities and respond big picture and long term." When you think this way, both as an individual and as an institution, you are more likely to act consistently and become more worthy of trust. Yes, you sometimes have to make short-term decisions, but even these decisions must be considered in a longer-term context. And yes, sometimes we have to make decisions that are narrow in scope, but even these decisions must be considered within the bigger picture. Think of yourself as operating along two axes—one measured by time and one measured by breadth.

Every setting is not high up in the ivory tower of academe. I get that. Public institutions, especially those that involve elected officials, are often criticized for making decisions and taking actions that are short in term and narrow in focus. Our question, then, becomes, how can elected officials and the institutions they lead adopt a long term, big-picture perspective when their measures of accountability—elections or business quarters—are so short in term and narrow in focus? Step one is to recognize the challenge. Short-termism especially is a real feature of decision making today—be it in politics, business, or even families, which are more indebted now than ever before. For many families, but not all, indebtedness sometimes stems from actions based on short-term thinking. Also recognize that the pressures forcing public institutions to think and act more in the short term and in a narrow focus are increasing. There is much more information available than ever before; it is circulating faster than ever before; and it demands that we make decisions more swiftly than ever before. We do not allow ourselves time to sift through the information we get and spend the time we need to consider it, as we did in the past—all of which tends to lead us to make decisions and take actions centred on the immediate and the narrow.

Equipped with this twin recognition, step two is to build and maintain institutions that give us the capacity to exercise sober second thought. This step is why I have always been a believer in our country's Senate, though my faith in that institution has been tested at times. The recent reforms to this legislative body—with clearer respect for the merit principle in appointments, and greater transparency and administrative rigour in its operations—are especially welcome, as they strengthen the Senate's power of sober second thought without giving it power equal to that of the House of Commons.

Keeping our division of head of state and head of government is another way to use our institutions to promote long-term and big-picture thoughts and acts. This set-up has served us well. Since the mid-nineteenth century and the advent of responsible government in British North America, Canada has enjoyed what Walter Bagehot called the dual Crown. The first aspect of this duality is the efficient Crown—which is elected and has the prime minister as head of government, and which passes laws, raises taxes, authorizes expenditures, and deploys armed forces. Given the nature of elections, continual polling of opinion, and the speed at which modern government is expected to work today, the efficient Crown is often under pressure to make short-term or expedient decisions.

The second aspect of this duality is the dignified Crown—which has a hereditary monarch (currently Queen Elizabeth II) as head of state and a representative in Canada (the governor general), who is appointed on recommendation by the prime minister to the monarch "to serve at her pleasure." The governor general not only ensures the country always has a prime minister and government that enjoy the confidence of the House of Commons but also prorogues and dissolves Parliament, safeguards the constitution and rule of law, and signs bills and instruments into law. The governor general, speaking with the prime minister in their private conversations, also has the right, according to Bagehot, to be consulted, to encourage, and to warn. The "warn" is the most delicate and nuanced of these responsibilities. Given its remove from the hurly-burly of modern politics, the dignified Crown can approach matters from a longer, more stable perspective, which allows for a wide range of interests to be considered and which provides a measure of calm.

Building and maintaining institutions that enable us to exercise the sober second thought that leads to consistency is why I am no fan of referenda as instruments of democracy for most matters. I dislike them for several specific reasons. One, referenda divide families—often irrevocably. Two, they usually focus on a single issue, which polarizes the country's family. Three, they are invariably emotional affairs—extremely so, which tends to cloud or distort our individual and collective thinking. Four, they are often short-term reactions to immediate events. And fifth, they have not gone through the filtering process of party platforms, election contests, and elected legislatures. That process almost always improves what is under consideration, almost always supplies citizens with more opportunities to shape what is under consideration, and almost always strengthens the public's trust in the institutions through which the shaping and improving occur.

Most of all, I am cautious about referenda because they have unintended consequences. In such a complex ecosystem of a country and society as ours, one simply cannot think through thoroughly what is going to happen as a result of the application of a question or resolution. Referenda are the very antithesis of long term and big picture, and they distort the complex and proven workings or interplay of our democracy. I think of the interplay between the partisan and nonpartisan aspects of our democracy as a gear that meshes together seamlessly and works together harmoniously to power the country's democratic machine. When one aspect of the gear is more powerful than the other, it torques the gear and drives the machine in an unfamiliar direction or causes the entire contraption to fly into chaos.

Money can have that same effect, overriding the harmony of that synchronized gear, especially when that money comes in substantial amounts from very specific interests and in secret. We often lament that the gear is slow to grind. Yet it is through its measured pace that the gear performs consistently, and it is through that consistency that trust arises and grows stronger.

Each of us as individuals should heed this example. Bring the same temperament and characteristics to our behaviour whether we are in public or private. Achieve such steady consistency of action that others' trust in us builds steadily and irreversibly. Arrive on foot, some might say.

5

Do the right thing, not just the thing right

Adhering to the moral imperative ahead of the operational
imperative builds and maintains trust.

Charles Dickens understood the value of doing the right thing
ahead of merely doing the thing right. At the centre of his novel
Bleak House, which was published as a serial over several months
during 1852 and 1853, is the court case of Jarndyce and Jarndyce.
The legal matter deals with a large inheritance whose disposition
has droned on for generations. The matter is finally resolved by
novel's end, but not before it has inflicted a cruel fate on each of
the main characters. As for the inheritance, it has been ground
down into the dirt, consumed by lawyers' fees.

This satire of English legal proceedings is laden with similar such cases in which the system and its professionals

operated according to accepted rules and practices—things were done right—but evidence of the right thing being done was nowhere in sight. (I think it was Voltaire who once observed, "I have been ruined twice: once when I lost a lawsuit and once when I won.")

Dickens's treatment of this case reminds me of a cruel joke in the medical profession: "The operation was successful, but the patient died." It points to the delusion of those who believe an operation can be carried out flawlessly from a technical perspective even though the patient in question dies.

I raise the example of *Bleak House* because professions and the people who practise them play fundamental roles in our society in strengthening trust by adhering to the moral imperative (doing the right thing) ahead of the operational imperative (doing the thing right). What is a profession and what does it mean to be a professional? One, a profession has a unique body of knowledge that is usually taught to budding professionals by accomplished ones. Part of this teaching and learning means all professionals—experienced and fledging— share a duty to build and extend knowledge and spur innovation—constant improvement—within the profession. Two, the profession controls entry, exit, and continuing competence. And third, the profession enjoys a social contract or public trust that gives professionals a monopoly to practise that profession. If the profession or individual professionals fail in some way, public trust in the profession weakens or erodes. If public trust erodes enough, the government or other public authority intervenes either to reassert the social contract or to constrain or remove the profession's monopoly control over the exercise of the profession.

Public trust writ large is the key. The state gives special status to a profession—be it the law or medicine or teaching—to take responsibility for the first two elements: knowledge and innovation, and membership. But if the profession does not live up to the social contract or public trust—the third element—then the state or monopoly-granter will amend or remove all these powers.

This principle goes back to the Middle Ages when the English Crown recognized guilds, which had a monopoly on entrance into a profession and those in the profession also taught it. (Or to stretch the point, perhaps the principle goes back even earlier to Socrates and his students.) I like to think of professions as both glue and grease. Professions serve vital functions that help hold a society together. When trust in a profession erodes, this glue dissolves and society is weakened. To mix my metaphors, professions also serve as grease that helps societies function more smoothly. When trust in a profession dissolves, friction results. If this trust dissolves completely, a society can grind to a halt, which leads to chaos and anarchy, conditions in which professional responsibilities do not mean much.

Professional bodies and the societies in which they operate avoid this type of behaviour through a combination of carrots and sticks. The main stick is to remove someone's licence as a professional or, if a transgression is flagrant enough, to use the criminal justice system to put that person in jail. The main carrot is to encourage professionals to do the right thing and not just the thing right.

Recognition through an honours system is a carrot. We all respond better to rewards for good behaviour than we do punishments for bad—professionals included. The best professional bodies astutely take advantage of human nature by showing professionals how doing the right thing strengthens public trust, advances the country, and enables professionals themselves to enjoy more rewarding careers and fulfilling lives.

While I was governor general, we employed what I call the voice of the office to encourage professionals to do the right thing. I spoke to many different groups of professionals—lawyers, physicians, engineers, and educators—about the central role they play in strengthening public trust. Some welcomed my remarks. A few others got their backs up—so much so that they asked me not to speak with them, or to change the subject. These groups basically said, "We would much rather hear you share your thoughts on our rights as professionals as opposed to our responsibilities."

For some professionals, the trust relationship can be a tricky one. Physicians and surgeons have a nationwide governing body that oversees ethics and certification. Yet these same physicians and surgeons have provincial bodies that handle collective bargaining of wages and conditions of work. Unless the ethics body and the bargaining bodies recognize their different mandates and work in harmony, the dialogue tends to become more about rights than collective responsibilities. Public trust erodes when the balance between professional ethics and bargaining tilts too much in the direction of bargaining.

Canadian professionals, by and large, succeed in doing the

right thing when compared to those in most other countries. What is behind that success? The answer stems from three sources. One, the educational system that produces professionals functions properly to teach professional skills and the ethics on which the practice of these skills are based. Two, Canadian professionals enjoy a strong ethic of directing their efforts to add to the public good. This ethic has been embedded deeply into many of our professions across generations of practice. And three, Canadians tend to think more as a collective than as individuals. For us, it is more about the welfare of the group than the survival of the fittest, and this attitude is fertile ground for strengthening professional ethics and public trust in professions.

Here is an example. The British Broadcasting Corporation, which is recognized as the standard-bearer for the world's public broadcasters, sent its top young strategy person to Canadian Broadcasting Corporation headquarters recently. While this professional was here, he met with some thirty Canadians from a variety of professions to try to understand why Canada is a more socially cohesive country than most others. He had several big questions to ask. Why do Canadians consider immigrants to be a plus? Why does Canada not have so many of the immigrant ghettos that exist in other countries? Why are there no great gaps in educational outcomes of native-born children and immigrant children? Why do immigrants have more trust in our public institutions than those of us who have multiple generations of Canadian-born forebears?

A number of factors contribute to our social cohesion. The first is our system of public education. We aspire to give everyone a decent opportunity to learn, grow, and succeed. The second is the programs we have put in place to increase the rate of high school graduation for students of immigrant families. And the third factor is the special attention we pay to help lower-income families fund their children's higher education. Both low-income and Indigenous examples suggest that everything is not fine, but these efforts are creating greater social cohesion and trust by giving new Canadians and lower-income citizens access to education and thereby enabling them to enjoy more social mobility than they would otherwise.

This approach finds its earliest expression in our country in the interaction between Indigenous people and the earliest settlers. Champlain's first settlers at Port Royal survived their first two winters because local Indigenous people supplied them with fresh meat to ward off malnutrition, as well as a tea made from evergreen needles to prevent disease, particularly what we later determined to be scurvy. The social cohesion that the BBC strategist came to study is the product of generations of thinking and behaving that has become embedded. And this social cohesion is simply another way of thinking about public trust—the trust we have in each other to do the right thing for all.

This propensity to adhere to the moral imperative ahead of the operational imperative is one important reason that Canadian banks and financial institutions weathered the 2008 financial storm so well. Yes, they fared well in part because of sound government regulation. Our banks are chartered federally, so we do not have a range of different rules and regulations across the country. That said, our bankers, for the most part, did not venture into esoteric financial instruments, and they were prudent enough generally to stay away from any financial instruments they did not understand. Underlying that prudence was a custom to avoid sharp practices with one another, with their institutional clients and, for the most part, with their individual customers. While Canadian banks are far from perfect in how they treat customers, they adhered to a strong ethical sense under which they had been operating for many decades.

Contrast that attitude with the one shown by Wells Fargo in the United States between 2011 and 2016. What happened there is a perfect illustration of what happens when doing the thing right trumps doing the right thing. At the time, many viewed Wells Fargo as perhaps the most successful retail bank in the United States—retail in the sense that it deals predominantly with individual consumers rather than large institutional clients. It also enjoyed a long and storied history that dates back to the Pony Express of the American West. Over these many decades, Wells Fargo built up a high level of client satisfaction and trust. Then the bank began to measure its success less on customer satisfaction and trust and more on the number of the bank's products held by each customer as a result of a practice known as cross-selling. The cross-selling became so pervasive that employees were encouraged to order credit cards for pre-approved customers without their consent. They also created fraudulent chequing and savings accounts and lines of credit, which sometimes involved employees moving money out of legitimate accounts. Creation of these additional accounts and other products was done in part through a process known as pinning, by which an employee would set a consumer's personal identification number to 0000. In this way, bankers were able to control client accounts and thereby enrol these clients in further programs.

The practice got so out of hand that Wells Fargo employees set up some 3.5 million fraudulent accounts before the scam was uncovered and hit the front pages. Although the bank's CEO claimed he did not know what was going on and that abhorrent behaviour was isolated, it turned out that the deception was so widespread and deep in the organization that the CEO ended up resigning.

How could this behaviour happen so widely and for so long? It took place because of a fixation on doing the thing right and a total disregard for doing the right thing. The company set up a system that became perverse because the conception of doing the right thing just was not strong enough to withstand a powerful incentive to do the thing right. The thing right was generating as much cross-selling as possible, racking up as many accounts as possible, charging as many fees as possible to customers, and for staff to earn as many commissions, bonuses, and rewards as possible.

In this sort of atmosphere, doing the right thing just disappeared. It conjures up Sir Walter Scott's iconic phrase: "Oh, what a tangled web we weave when first we practise to deceive." The corporate code of conduct that Wells Fargo employees signed each year went out the window. I am sure some fine lawyers drafted the code of conduct and that it said all the right things. I presume too that the human resources folks at Wells

Fargo made certain that employees signed the code each year. But what good did all that do? You can lead a horse to water, but you can't make it drink.

Lawyers in Victorian England and bankers in twenty-first-century America are not the only professionals to prioritize doing the thing right over doing the right thing. Engineers at Volkswagen also have been guilty of this practice. In January 2017, the company pleaded guilty to criminal charges and signed a statement of facts that described how it had sold many diesel-engine cars in the United States that were fitted with so-called defeat devices—or software—that could detect when these vehicles were being tested and change their performance accordingly to improve emissions results and meet environmental standards. Theirs was a brilliant feat of engineering—and of moral failure. Several Volkswagen Group senior executives have since resigned or been suspended for their roles in rigging diesel-powered vehicles to cheat on government emissions tests. And four months after Volkswagen pleaded guilty, a U.S. federal judge ordered the company to pay a $2.8 billion criminal fine.

The massive penalty shows how doing the thing right over doing the right thing can have significant bottom-line consequences. More importantly, the example of Volkswagen and those from different professions and industries show that to build and maintain trust, organizations cannot merely make a passing nod at doing the right thing. They must cultivate and entrench a culture that stresses doing the morally right thing ahead of doing the thing right mechanically; they must nurture a culture that places the moral imperative ahead of the operational imperative.

Organizations create this culture by leading from the top and expressing that leadership by communicating often and widely, and making sure that culture is owned by all. They have to say it, and then they have to act on it every day. Case closed.

6

Rise above the written rules

Laws grounded in fairness and informed by wisdom
enable us to strive toward justice, the pursuit of which fosters hope,
dispels despair, and elevates trust.

If I were opening a law school, I would carve two questions in
stone at its entrance: "Is law just?" and just below the first, "Is the
particular law you are applying just?" These questions go to the
heart of my thinking about the distinction between law and justice. The rule of law is trusted only if the laws that make up the
overall body of jurisprudence are grounded in fairness, informed
by wisdom, and thereby move a society closer to justice. Law is a
statement of fact, a rule. Justice is a system of values.

To answer these two fundamental questions, one first must
know the particular law under question, why that law came into

being, and whether that law was considered just or unjust according to the values of the time when it was introduced. If it were considered just, as most laws are when introduced originally according to then current values, one must then determine how values have changed that might now render the law unjust or not fully just.

That is the second point: Is it just today? Legal professionals have a responsibility to make sure laws meet this perpetual test. Lawyers take an oath "to improve the administration of justice." This oath requires them to try to change any law they happen to be working on when it no longer meets the requirements of justice or did not in the first place. I realize lawyers—unless they are legislators, law professors, or members of a law reform commission—cannot be expected to spend their every waking hour improving laws. Nonetheless, lawyers should see their responsibility to rise above the written rules and strive toward justice.

This idea of rising above the written rules deserves our consideration separate from doing the right thing because the rule of law grounded in justice is a principle of bedrock importance to democracy in Canada. To be more precise, the written rules of law are a subset of doing the right thing, or a way of going about doing the right thing. We can elevate that idea of doing the right thing to an even higher plane by using our laws—individually and as a body—to propel us closer to justice. We must do so, however, in the knowledge that we will never achieve absolute justice in any aspect of our country's life. That is just too elusive an ideal. But its pursuit should always remain a primary goal in our democracy.

When I think about the rule of law as a principle of fundamental importance to democracy in Canada, and how the rule of law and democracy are founded on the bedrock element of trust, I return to my days as an undergraduate at Harvard when these ideas first began to percolate. Like many young people then, I first appreciated the difference between mere laws and the pursuit of justice from the perspective of an athlete. I saw how rules listed on the page differed from how they were interpreted and applied on the diamond, field, or rink. I also saw how their interpretation and application could change from game to game and even during the course of a game. My understanding of this interplay between intent, interpretation, and application has evolved over the many years since, moving from the playing field to other aspects of life.

An early, formative moment in my understanding took place when I was a student at Harvard. I recall vividly a course taught by Reinhold Niebuhr. He was a celebrated Christian theologian and ethicist who approached most questions from the perspective of love thy neighbour, but with an understanding that some neighbours are going to require a different and perhaps more hard-fisted approach to keep them in line. One of Niebuhr's cherished axioms is "Man's capacity for justice makes democracy possible; but man's inclination to injustice makes democracy necessary." I interpret this sentence as meaning that rules alone are not enough to protect societies from cynicism, corruption, and injustice. It is necessary for citizens to rise above the rules and strive always toward justice.

To strive, we need to see fairness in the construct and desired outcome of a law. Only then can we see laws as instruments to

achieve justice that fosters hope, dispels despair, and elevates trust. If a law divides and excludes, it will drive us away from
justice. If a law is too complex for us to see whether it is grounded in fairness, its opaqueness will blind us to justice. We also need to discern in a law the coupling of fairness with wisdom that comes from careful consideration and experience. Trust is tested and maintained only when governments, legislatures, and courts develop, interpret, and apply rules that are predicated on fairness and informed by wisdom.

The need to rise above the rules and strive toward justice is more important today than ever before. One reason for the resurgence in nativism and populism in many places in the Western world is that many people perceive that too many technically correct and so-called intelligent rules are rigged in favour of the wealthy and the powerful. Many people look at tax and financial rules and free trade agreements and say, "This isn't fair. These intelligent rule-writers are writing laws and agreements that are costing me my job." Populist movements in countries around the world are fuelled in large part by the belief that the law does not really represent the individual citizens and is leaving them behind. We must remind ourselves that while the law as written must be viewed as fair, trust takes flight if interpretation and application of that law as written have become such that fairness has faded and vanished.

The Second Amendment to the United States Constitution illustrates this point. The amendment states: "A well-regulated militia being necessary to the security of a free state, the right of the people to keep and bear arms shall not be infringed."

Remember, this amendment became law shortly after the Thirteen Colonies won their independence from Great Britain and King George III by defeating the British Army. Before the American Revolution, Britain billeted its troops, bearing arms, in the homes of the colonists, who had, at best, very few or somewhat archaic firearms. When adopted and for several generations after, therefore, the amendment was interpreted by citizens, legislatures, and courts as a protection of the citizen against an oppressive state that used its force of arms against the interest of the individual. The amendment was intended to make it possible for that individual and his or her neighbours to raise an armed militia to defend themselves against a force that they deemed to be tyrannical or illegitimate.

This meaning has changed over two centuries to become interpreted as giving every citizen the right to own and often openly carry virtually any kind of armed weapon, including arms usually reserved for law enforcement agencies and branches of the military in active combat. As its interpretation and application changed, this legal principle became an individual freedom or right that permitted the citizen not only to protect himself or herself against an oppressive state, but also an "oppressive" neighbour. This "oppression" can range from an unlawful neighbour who steals from you to a neighbour who looks at you the wrong way as you walk down the street.

I exaggerate, but that is the path down which this amendment has travelled. Interpretation of the law in this way leads to a society in which people place a growing trust in themselves to exercise force and administer justice, and a diminishing trust in officials of the state who possess a monopoly of force and whose job it is to keep people safe. This kind of deliberate diminution of trust in the instruments of the state has a corrosive effect on overall trust in a society. It speaks to an every-man-for-himself mentality that is the very negation of public trust. It is the opposite of rising above the written rules. Rather, it is an undermining of the written rule by turning it, through interpretation and application, into something that it is not.

An example of a court that rises above a wooden interpretation of the written rules to strive toward justice and build trust is our own Supreme Court. Shortly after finishing my term as governor general, I had the privilege of speaking at the farewell dinner for Chief Justice of the Supreme Court of Canada Beverley McLachlin. I believe Chief Justice McLachlin and her court will be regarded by historians as one of Canada's most distinguished and influential groups of jurists, as well as among the most admired courts in the world. I spoke of three things: the Canadian constitution, the Supreme Court, and the Chief Justice herself.

About the constitution, I said that over the years as a law student and professor I saw the Canadian constitution emerge from a position of obscurity to be one of the most respected governmental frameworks in the world. The product of some thousand years of legal history, the Canadian constitution is one of the most satisfactory frameworks of government, as measured by the degree of trust that its citizens have in it and its success in bringing about fairness among these citizens. But the Canadian constitution's success flows from much more than its written rules. When Walter Bagehot—who founded *The Economist* magazine in the mid-nineteenth century and who wrote extensively about government theory and practice—was told that the United States constitution was the most wonderful document struck by the hand of man, he replied, "Nonsense. The men of Massachusetts could make any document work."

Which brings me to the Supreme Court of Canada. The strength of the Canadian constitution is that it has been interpreted and administered as a "living tree" by people who have had the particular wisdom to value fairness, avoid extremes, and recognize the dignity of each individual. The Supreme Court of Canada—the McLachlin court especially—and the lower courts that followed its precedents have displayed what I call a "measured boldness" in interpreting the written rules of the constitution. Boldness in that the Supreme Court sees the law as a mechanism to achieve justice, and measured in that the court realizes its fallibility, as well as the legislative authority of Parliament, and therefore its duty to approach its goal with care.

Also at the dinner were the two people who appointed Chief Justice McLachlin to the court and to the position of Chief Justice. Prime Minister Brian Mulroney appointed Beverley McLachlin to the Supreme Court in 1989. A relatively young and unknown law professor and British Columbia Court of Appeal Judge, she was the second woman to be appointed to the court. Eleven years later, Prime Minister Jean Chrétien named her the first woman to be the court's chief justice. I saluted these prime ministers and those who have followed for ensuring that those named to the bench come from the highest ranks of the legal profession—that merit was the paramount criterion. These decision makers understood the importance of choosing our finest and wisest people to interpret the law. This is a fundamental element in building trust in the legal system, choosing justices using a scrupulous, merit-based approach.

Which brings me to Chief Justice McLachlin herself, who led the court with measured boldness and a collegial capacity to cultivate the very best from those working with and around her. In my remarks at Chief Justice McLachlin's farewell dinner, I identified two areas of law in which the McLachlin court is particularly distinguished. The first is its interpretation of the Charter of Rights and Freedoms. When the Charter was adopted in 1982, many critics were convinced it could not work. They said it was a hodgepodge that mixed the existing Westminster system—which has been built from the ground up in British common law and the sovereignty of Parliament—with a new entrenched bill of rights. These rights were created from the top down by declaratory principles established in European civil law, which in turn was built on the declamations of Roman law. Add to the mix the fact that an unelected court would interpret these rights and could override—render null and void—the sovereign will of the people as expressed through their Parliament.

These critics, however, may have forgotten that, in 1774 with the Quebec Act, Canada brought together civil law and common law, as the French-speaking and English-speaking peoples of the colony formed their compact. That agreement remains fundamental to Canada's constitutional culture. Since then, the country has made these two great legal traditions of Western civilization work together. The measured boldness that the Supreme Court has shown since 1982 has enabled the Charter to fit comfortably within the Canadian constitution. At the same time, the Charter has become an important educational tool, something each Canadian can clutch in the hand and say, "This is my protection from an overbearing state or wilful majority."

The McLachlin court's second area of distinction has been its capacity to weave a new garment of Indigenous law using the principles of the Charter. The court had to operate in this way, what legal professionals call *in terra nulla*, because the former legal environment gave very little legislative guidance, due to the inability of legislatures across the country to craft laws that bring about basic fairness for Indigenous people in Canada, and due to the fact that precedents from many other jurisdictions were based on the law of conquest.

Even with the efforts of the McLachlin court, we remain a long way from achieving justice for Indigenous peoples in our country. Yet inspired by reconciliation and guided by the court's fair and wise interpretation of the Charter, Canadians are rising above the written rules and, in so doing, are strengthening trust in the country.

7

Find some faith

Service and belonging to a wider world is the
passport to a life of greater fulfillment and trust.

Faith takes many forms. It can be associated with organized religions. It can be a personal spirituality. And it can be entirely
secular. Whatever your faith, it is a wellspring of trust.

Christianity has been my rock for my whole life. I grew up in
northern Ontario in the Anglican tradition and went to my
neighbourhood church every Sunday. As a choirboy and altar boy,
I learned the Gospel, absorbed the wisdom of the Prophets, and
sang hymns that expressed the trials and triumphs of a godly life.
If my schools nurtured my curiosity and my community gave me
support, my church made it possible for me to imagine a world
and an approach to life that was greater than my own and yet one
that stemmed from my own.

My faith remained strong as I reached adulthood and left my hometown of Sault Ste. Marie to attend university. While at Harvard, I took the short course at Episcopal Theological College, which adjoined the university campus, to become a lay reader. In the Anglican Church, a lay reader is a person who is qualified to preach and conduct some religious services, but not licensed to officiate over baptisms, marriages, funerals, and Holy Communion.

This knowledge gave me yet another window to the world. For several summers, I filled in on Sundays for the Anglican ministers who served in several First Nations reserves and two rural parishes near my hometown. These services were my first in-depth encounters with First Nations people, opening my eyes still again to a world and approach to life that were broader than my own, and yet a world and approach that stemmed from my own and were recognizable in my own.

Faith was and remains my passport to these experiences and understanding. Through the practice of my faith, I realize my limitations and even my powerlessness in some circumstances. I gain a willingness to explore and understand better the condition and lives of others. Most importantly, faith enables me to move beyond my individualism and recognize my obligation to my community, country, and world. It teaches me to understand that I am more than my own success and happiness. My success and happiness is closely and irrevocably tied to the success and happiness of the world around me, and the people who make up that world—family, friends, neighbours, and fellow citizens.

That is the power I have discovered in finding and having faith. In equipping me with this understanding and approach, I believe my faith has made me more worthy of trust from others. It has also enabled me to spot others who are worthy of my trust. Queen Elizabeth II is one of these people. I am not alone in making this assessment: Her Majesty is one of the most trusted public figures in the world and has been for much of her adult life. I believe much of the trust people have for Her Majesty stems from her faith, which she displays publicly and with dignity.

Her Majesty's undisguised demonstration of her faith began early in life. In the foreword she wrote to *The Servant Queen and the King She Serves*, Her Majesty refers to a poem quoted by her father, King George VI, in his Christmas broadcast in 1939. Think of the time: Europe found itself at war for the second time in just over a generation; the invasion of Britain seemed an imminent peril; and the King, who had to work to overcome a debilitating stammer, had been thrust onto the throne only two years earlier, surprised and unprepared after the abdication of his older brother, Edward VIII.

The poem Her Majesty mentions—and that her father recited nearly eighty years ago—is brief:

I said to the man who stood at the Gate of the Year:
Give me a light that I may tread safely in the unknown.
And he replied, Go out into the darkness, and put your hand into
    the hand of God;
That shall be to you better than light and safer than a known way.

So I went forth, and finding the Hand of God, trod gladly into the night.

And He led me towards the hills and the breaking of day in the lone East.

What is less known is the name of the person who made King George aware of the poem. It was the future Queen, Princess Elizabeth, the King's then-thirteen-year-old daughter. Typical of Her Majesty's habit of shining a light on the ideas and achievements of others, this item of information is not contained in her foreword to *The Servant Queen* but is disclosed later in the book by its author. This revelation, however, does make clear how rooted and ever-present Her Majesty's faith has been in her life.

What may be surprising, yet wholly in keeping with her faith, Her Majesty's strong Christian beliefs do not lead her to exclude other faiths or people who choose not to ascribe to an organized religious faith. Just the opposite: Her Majesty's faith inspires her to respect beliefs other than her own, and to accord these faiths and those who hold them dear the same dignity she grants to those who share her faith.

Her example is an important lesson in social trust for people of different faiths and those of no religious faith. As Jonathan Sacks, former Chief Rabbi of the United Hebrew Congregations of the Commonwealth, said: "We do not always appreciate the role the Queen has played in the transformation of Britain into a multi-ethnic, multi-faith society. Her presence and family role as the human face of national identity is one of the great unifying forces in Britain, a unity we need the more diverse religiously and culturally we become."

Rabbi Sacks raises something important about trust and its connection to faith. As Canada and other democracies become more diverse culturally and religiously, each of us can use faith to find common ground and earn trust through this bond. For me that common ground is humility, in the sense that I do not have all the answers and no one religious faith is absolute. Humility also means I am no better than anyone else: we are all deserving of love, mercy, and grace from whatever power put us here on this planet and, more importantly, from each other. This way of looking at life applies to people of all faiths or of no organized religious order. In this spirit, we must never permit our religious faiths to inspire us to thoughts and actions of pride and intolerance. Our faiths should be our guides and not absolute truths. They should motivate us to love and serve others; they should open us to ever-larger circles of community and belonging; and, in inspiring us to serve and in opening us to larger worlds, our faiths make us more worthy of trust.

Yet religious belief is not the only article of faith that can serve as the basis for this trust. The faith that enables each of us to move beyond the borders of our individual worlds and recognize our obligation to something bigger takes many forms—as many forms as there are people. One such form is that practised by a dear friend of mine, who is one of the most intelligent and unselfish people I have ever known. He has no faith that stems from organized religion. His creed is medicine and Mozart. Medicine gives him an academic and professional medium through which he can channel his hard-won knowledge and skills in the service of others, while the exquisite artistic talent of another person—in this case, the music of Wolfgang Amadeus Mozart—not only comforts and inspires him, but also connects him instantly with a community of fellow worshippers that spans centuries of time and immeasurable distance. The music of Mozart, like all sublime artistic achievement, also tends to move my friend as though he were experiencing something divine or at least otherworldly. Such is the power of art.

This combination of service and belonging is a form of faith. After all, service to others is a central if not the foremost quality of all organized religions. My friend's articles of faith, like all religions, also enable him to belong to something larger and more meaningful than his own existence and, in the process, make his life richer and more consequential. That is the power of faith, and that is how those who have found a faith build trust.

French novelist Victor Hugo wrote that a faith is a necessity to man and therefore woe to him who believes in nothing. I say, woe to those who believe in nothing beyond their individual world. So find some faith. I found mine in the Anglican church, as did Her Majesty Queen Elizabeth II. Yours can stem from an organized religion, a personal spirituality, or from anything that, like my friend's, makes it possible for you to serve a calling and belong to a community greater than you alone.

When you do find it, not only will your life become richer, more meaningful, and more fulfilling, but you will also become more worthy of trust in the eyes of others. And that is something we all can believe in together.

8

Follow the Golden Rule

Doing unto others as you would have them
do unto you is a determinant and test of trust.

The Golden Rule is a fundamental determinant of trusting relationships. When a person lives this centuries-old axiom, he or
she builds trust with other people. When communities of people
emphasize the rule, collective trust grows and these communities
thrive as a result. And when businesses, organizations, and public
institutions do unto people as the individuals who make up these
groups would have done unto themselves, they engender trust
and endure. The power of the Golden Rule is empathy—seeing
your neighbour as yourself and acting accordingly.

Equipped with this understanding, any human goal of positive
collaborative interaction is within reach. Without it, any

relationship is doomed to fail in time. Simply put, permanent human gatherings of any size would not be able to function without basic empathy and reciprocity among the people who make up the gathering. Another feature that makes this principle so attractive is that any person and any organization can practise it: it is easy for anyone and any group to make living the Golden Rule part of their personal and institutional lives.

The straightforward nature of the Golden Rule should not lead anyone to believe that the principle is banal or time-worn or lacking in wisdom. While governor general, I participated in the opening of a particularly memorable conference on innovation. I remained at the gathering after I had delivered my speech because I wanted to hear what another participant—Robert Shiller—had to say. To my great surprise, the Nobel Prize–winning economist did not speak about the latest findings on finance, markets, or economics, or on his recent work in behavioural finance. Instead, he talked about what contributes most to what he called the good society.

According to Dr. Shiller, if one looks at the world's major religions, they all have at their core the Golden Rule. Our religious beliefs—regardless of where they emerge and what group of people they cluster around—are grounded in this principle. Surely, he argued, there is some guidance we can draw from this fact that we can apply to our own lives here and now.

His audience was riveted: here was this man, a legend in the field of economics, who believes not merely that there are more important things in life than the closing value of the Dow Jones Industrial Average, but more so that something so human as the

Golden Rule must complement and even expand our empirical knowledge. At first, I was simply surprised that this eminent academic would be inclined to use a conference on innovation to discuss something so philosophical. But then I asked myself: What good are even our most significant scientific findings if they are not understood or used in the context of serving this planet and those who dwell on it?

The experience reinforced my belief that how we treat each other individually and in groups is both a determinant and a test of trust. The *World Happiness Report* does a particularly good job of making the connection between treatment and trust. The annual report is a regular measure of happiness that is published by the United Nations Sustainable Development Solutions Network. University of British Columbia professor emeritus John Helliwell—another economist, as well as an officer of the Order of Canada—is editor of the report, and a founder of the idea that happiness should be the measure by which we gauge the performance of governments and the progress of countries and peoples.

Personal trust and institutional trust lie at the heart of the report's methodology. Personal trust is measured, among other things, by generosity and the degree to which people believe they can count on someone else in times of trouble. We are happier when we know we live in a society in which people care for one another and show that caring through their generosity and being there with support when others fall on hard times. Both measures are the very definition of doing unto others as you would have them do unto you. Institutional trust is measured by the amount of corruption in businesses and governments. Less is more. We are happier when we know we live in a society in which our private and public institutions behave honestly, honourably, and in harmony with the public interest, and not in the interest of the people who happen to occupy positions of authority or a small group within the public realm.

What Dr. Helliwell and his colleagues have done with the *World Happiness Report* is truly remarkable. Their work takes what has been for millennia an intangible philosophical question—What is happiness?—and turns it into an empirical matter we can gauge and track, and from which we can build good societies. The conclusion is clear: happy societies are trusting societies—both socially and institutionally—and trusting societies are happy societies. It is mutually reinforcing. Equally important, the methodology behind the report gives us a clear understanding of the social engineering we need to carry out—at home, at work, at play, and in our civic and democratic lives—to increase happiness and build trust.

This essential research into the link between giving, happiness, and trust inspired our work at Rideau Hall. From the very start of my mandate as governor general, we at Rideau Hall emphasized philanthropy, or giving, as a shared Canadian value that we wanted to bring to life among every person in every corner of the country. We did so not only because of the importance of giving, but also because we believed that the nonpartisan Office of the Governor General was an ideal place from which to carry out this work. To focus and make permanent our efforts to promote giving in Canada, we created the Rideau Hall

Foundation. This charitable organization, which is connected to the Office of the Governor General, has made it possible for us—together with our partners—to launch campaigns to promote giving and other shared Canadian values.

My Giving Moment was the first campaign. It was designed to encourage and celebrate giving—in all its forms—among young Canadians. While the effort was a great success, it showed us that giving was changing and that the ways in which people are choosing to give have become complex. As a result, we decided that while we undertook further public campaigns, we also needed to gain a much better understanding of what motivates people to give today, what the barriers to giving are, and what giving strategies and tactics are the most effective ones to pursue.

Our desire for answers led us to create the Giving Behaviour Project. The first research activity we carried out through the project was to analyze data from the past thirty years to understand clearly how giving has changed. We found that our country relies on an aging cohort of donors who are giving more and more. But what happens to giving in Canada when these givers pass on? The indications are worrisome, as younger generations are not grasping the mantle from that aging cohort of givers. This finding suggests younger generations do not consider giving to be a crucial Canadian value, or perhaps it reflects an emerging reality in which younger Canadians are finding alternative ways to connect and give to the causes that mean the most to them. Social media platforms such as GoFundMe appear to occupy major roles in the future of giving. What does this trend mean for the charitable sector in Canada and to giving, happiness, and trust?

We are exploring this question, too. The Rideau Hall Foundation has partnered with Proof, the Canadian communications company that surveys trust in Canada, to launch research into how millennials think about, learn about, and go about giving. In tandem with this work, we are examining what innovations may be brought to bear to encourage a stronger culture of giving in Canada, especially among young people. I believe there is some very exciting potential in applying the principles of behavioural sciences to encourage giving and in doing so generate more happiness and trust in the country.

Doing unto others as you would have them do unto you is not only a contributor to trust but also a test of trust. The Syrian refugee crisis was a telling moment for our country. I got a first-hand understanding of the gravity of the crisis when I travelled to Jordan in 2016 on an official visit to that country, as well as to Israel and the Palestinian Authority. During our visit, we visited the Zaatari refugee camp near Jordan's northern border with Syria. One of several camps that have emerged as the crisis intensified, Zaatari is now home to some 75,000 refugees and has evolved from a temporary encampment to a semi-permanent settlement. As a result of this experience, I made a point of calling John McCallum the day after he was sworn in as minister of immigration, refugees, and citizenship. I told him how happy I was for him and asked whether our office, with its convening power, could do anything to help with the integration into our country of the thousands of Syrian refugees that his government had pledged to welcome. He observed that the task was a daunting one, that he would appreciate any help our office could provide, and that he was open to any suggestions. I proposed convening a conference at Rideau Hall that included all the groups involved in handling Syrian refugees, particularly those groups leading private sponsorships of refugee families, which is an approach that is unique to Canada. The gathering would enable the groups to meet face to face, exchange ideas, and strategize about how the process could work better and be sustained. It would also shine a public spotlight on the crisis and the actions Canada was taking—to declare, in effect, this is something that is important for our country to do.

So we had the conference and it was a spectacular success. It was the first time many of these key players had actually seen one another. They were also able to comprehend the different parts that made up the whole process and how that process would work if it were to be successful. After the conference, we decided we would use the convening power in yet another way: We would celebrate some of the communities that had done a notable job in welcoming and integrating Syrian refugees.

One of these communities was Oakville, Ontario. We gathered one evening in a local auditorium with about five hundred volunteers engaged in making private sponsorships work in their town. The evening began with a Protestant minister, Catholic priest, rabbi and imam delivering a blessing on the event and those gathered there. I got up afterward to say a few words. I said how lovely it was to hear a blessing from representatives of several of Canada's religious traditions. I also pointed out that the congregations of these religions sponsored many refugee families. To be clear, I said, the four congregations, as one group, sponsored the families. They pooled not only their financial resources but also the best of their other resources as one unified multireligious group. The members of the mosque, with their knowledge of the language of the refugees, took on responsibility for communications. The synagogue made sure the young people were integrated into local schools. The Catholics looked after securing homes for the refugees. The Protestants worked on finding them jobs. And so forth. They were living the Golden Rule and their collective action is symbolic of Canada at its best: several religious traditions—at odds in so many other parts of the world—came together to do unto others as they would have others do unto them.

Some voices in our country were raised against this effort—a few even declaring that future terrorists were using the crisis as an opportunity to infiltrate the country. Yet the country took steps to mitigate this risk. The United Nations Human Rights Commission recommended to Canada refugees whom the commission had identified as legitimate and the most needy. Our country also sent our own security people to the refugee camps to screen prospective refugees. And we made a point not to take single men. The refugees coming to Canada were the most vulnerable people we could find. It is highly unlikely someone in this group would be willing to spend years in a refugee camp just so they could insert themselves into Canada and carry out a terrorist act.

The crisis tested our trust in another way. Some voices said that our country's cities have more than enough homeless people who are looking for roofs over their heads. They said: Why should we concentrate our efforts and resources on finding homes for people from abroad when we have so many in need already? My answer to that question—and many others like it— is that our response need not be an either-or proposition or a zero-sum game. There is nothing stopping Canadians from succeeding in doing both when we heed—if I may borrow Abraham Lincoln's words—the better angels of Canadian nature.

Canada's response to the Syrian refugee crisis appealed to these better angels of generosity and determination to support others in times of trouble. Yet these better angels are not merely metaphoric. They are qualities that increase happiness and strengthen trust for all Canadians—those born in this country and those newly arrived on its shores. Golden.

Part 2

Build trust around you

Six ways to think and act that will engender trust
in your communities, businesses, and organizations

9

Show up, not off

Being present establishes rapport, breaks down hierarchy,
and creates solidarity and trust around a shared cause.

Give me one teammate who shows up rather than ten who show off. I am confident that anyone who has participated in team sports agrees with me on this score. We have all had teammates who like to swagger and talk about how great they are—the show-offs. And we have all had teammates who just quietly but intently focus on getting the puck in the other team's net (and do not over-celebrate when they do) and keeping it out of their own. They are the steady ones who show up and do the work for the simple yet immense satisfaction of doing that work well.

Successful teams are built on players who show up, and other players and fans have pretty good antennae for determining which ones show up and which ones show off. Just as the best teammates do, the best leaders in business, organizations, and public institutions show up. They do so for a basic and important reason: to make clear to everyone on the team that the mission everyone has embarked upon is a collective effort that they will succeed in fulfilling only if they work together. Leaders also make a point to show up during trying situations and at difficult times, not just when cheering and celebrating is called for.

The ways in which leaders actually do the showing up are many. I have found the best way to show up is simply being present, especially when the heat is rising. A leader does not have to prove to everyone every day how smart he or she is, or demonstrate that he or she has the answer to every question and the solution to every problem. A leader does not show up these ways. Simply by being present, a leader establishes rapport with team members, breaks down the barriers of hierarchy, and creates solidarity and trust around a shared cause.

A straightforward way to show up is by going to people rather than having them come to you. I looked for as many opportunities as I could find to apply this approach while I served as governor general. My behaviour stemmed from an overall attitude of realism in this position. I know it is a role of authority and I had to demonstrate leadership and apply whatever wisdom I had gained over the years to carry out the role. Yet I also realized that I could not get carried away and think that I was something other than an ordinary person serving for a relatively short period of time in an extraordinary public institution. I still needed to be able to sit down with people, look them in the eye, say hello, and then get down to business.

So the custom we developed at Rideau Hall was that when I needed to see someone, I would usually walk through the building to see that person where he or she worked. I would not have people summoned to my office. I would also make a point of stopping by the office or workstation of any new employees to say hello and welcome them to the team. Again, I preferred this approach to having a representative call that person to my office, which felt too much like an audience. What I really wanted to do was greet and get to know something about a member of our team.

I would also try to place as many of my own phone calls as I could. I know it does not sound like much, but you would be surprised by how many organizational and hierarchical barriers get put up around people when they get placed at the head of a large public institution. I did not want to be placed in a protective bubble. There is also a natural tendency to let the entitlements of any position of authority go to your head—even among the most down-to-earth people. I tried, therefore, only to stand on ceremony during the more formal occasions. An excessive sense of entitlement and hierarchy can prevent trust from being strengthened, if not break it down altogether.

Another simple showing-up step we took at Rideau Hall was to make it a regular practice to eat lunch at the cafeteria on site. And it was not just me who took this step. Members of the institution's senior executive team would make sure that we did not book appointments for lunch every day. We never really

83
—

discussed it as a group. It was an action that came about more by inclination.

Truth be told, the governor general eating lunch in the Rideau Hall cafeteria was considered for years to be a breach of convention. Although I am someone who almost always abides by tradition, I was happy to skirt this one, because I saw joining the other members of the team for lunch as a straightforward way to establish rapport with the people I depended on every day. Together with the other executives, we wanted to establish in the minds of everyone at Rideau Hall that there was not a substantial separation between those of us who had the fancy titles and those who were carrying out the heavy lifting that kept the place going.

I did the same thing when I served as principal of McGill University. Some of my predecessors never entered the faculty club. They believed in the military separation of officers and enlisted personnel, and brought that same attitude to the university. As a mark in their favour, they believed noncommissioned officers (or faculty members in this case) needed private places of their own in which they could be free to meet and talk without feeling they were being overheard or cowed in any way by their superiors. Again, while I am usually a supporter of tradition, I do not favour it at the cost of team unity and trust.

Each of these actions on its own is not a grand deal in the great scheme of things, but these kinds of small acts have a cumulative effect on other people's attitudes toward you. Visiting people, calling them up directly on the phone, sitting down for lunch in the same gathering place—they are ways to establish rapport, break down hierarchy, and create solidarity around a shared cause. And all these outcomes build up, maintain, and strengthen trust.

All that said, I must confess that I did not always show up the way I wanted to while serving as governor general. Since I was sensitive to how my presence, by virtue of my office, had a tendency to focus the attention of any gathering on me, I occasionally made a misstep. One such misstep I remember most vividly occurred in the first few days of my tenure. Peter Mansbridge of cbc News asked me during a televised interview whether I would wear a uniform of the Canadian Forces while I was in office. I had not thought deeply about his question at that point. I should have, but I had not. So I was stumped for an answer and ended up responding in a highly equivocal way. If I remember correctly, I said, "Probably not." How is that for decisive! He was kind enough not to challenge me by saying, "But come on, man, you're commander in chief!"

My thinking at the time was that I should not wear the uniform of our country's armed forces because I had not earned the right to wear it and therefore I did not want to usurp or assume as my own the dignity and commitment of the people who had earned that right. I would be bearing false witness. I would be showing off.

A month after the interview, I travelled to Afghanistan to show my respect for the men and women who were serving there with such integrity and bravery. I wore combat fatigues throughout my time in Afghanistan, as everyone had to do when they were there. Near the end of my visit, General Walt

Natynczyk, chief of the defence staff, said to me, "Sir, that uniform looks pretty good on you. I hope you'll wear it as often as

you can, particularly on formal occasions." I replied, "General, if you are asking me on behalf of the men and women of the Canadian Forces, then I will do so as often as I can and with great pride."

And I did. I would also wear, as often as possible, the neckties of the three regiments that make up the Governor General's Guards. As I reflect on the whole matter now, I realize that I should not have been so hesitant about wearing the uniform, fearing I would be showing off. I was making my decision on the standpoint of me as a person and not as the country's governor general and commander in chief of Canada's armed forces. I let my desire to not show off override what was really my professional duty to show up. Wearing the uniform was a case in which I needed to be present in the appropriate way, and I am thankful to Walt Natynczyk, who is an outstanding leader and has become a close friend, for so kindly yet directly helping me find my footing.

Once I did so, I became part of a vivid illustration of showing up: the repatriation ceremony for men and women who were killed while deployed in Afghanistan. The initial practice for Canadians who were killed in action in Afghanistan had been for the casket to be flown into Trenton Air Force Base, where a ramp ceremony would be held. Gathered there would be the immediate family of the serviceman or servicewoman who had been killed in action, along with a very small group of the immediate comrades of the deceased. And no one else. The captains and

colonels would not be there. The chief of the defence staff would
not be there. The prime minister and defence minister would not
be there. And the governor general would not be there. It was
intended to be a private and sorrowful occasion on which the
people closest to the deceased would pay their last respects to
their family member or comrade in arms.

As we began to see casualties increase, senior officers of the
military and representatives of the government (including my
predecessors as governor general) changed the policy from one
in which the brass stayed home to one in which the brass
showed up. They made this decision because they believed that
these losses not only were personal ones, but also were losses to
the national family. When we lose one of our men and women
in uniform, it is a national tragedy and therefore the nation
should be represented and mourn. As senior people in the
nation's hierarchy, we needed to show up in difficult situations
and at difficult times. In particular, it was the minister of
defence—on behalf of cabinet—who decided these military
personnel must go to Afghanistan; it was the chief of the
defence staff who ordered them to go; and it is the governor
general who is titular commander in chief of the country's
armed forces. The presence of these officials at repatriation ceremonies was meant to show solidarity with that person and that
person's family and close comrades. The immediate family had
the option to decline that larger showing up, although that
never happened during my time as governor general. I think in
many instances it changed the view of that family. They, too,
saw the loss as not only a personal one but also a national one;

representatives by their very presence were there to say that it was a national loss.

My wife, Sharon, and I showed up at all repatriation ceremonies that took place on our watch. We would steel ourselves emotionally to try to be helpful and supportive to the families of the fallen. Yet I was always amazed at how the families would reach out to us—to support and comfort us. We went there to be the comforters and we ended up being the comforted. For his part, Walt Natynczyk, the chief of the defence staff, told me that he and his wife, Leslie, felt they had a moral obligation to be there. In fact, Walt told me there was no other place where they should be at those times.

From this change came the custom that, even though ramp ceremonies were closed to the public, crowds would be four or five deep on the other side of the fence at Trenton, observing in respectful silence. The body in the casket would then be transported by motor cortege to a forensic lab in Toronto for an autopsy, after which the family would take possession of the body. As the cortege proceeded down the portion of Highway 401 now known as the Highway of Heroes, the overpasses were lined with people paying their respects to these fallen soldiers. They would bow their heads and some would salute as the cars passed under them. Cars travelling the other way on the highway would pull over to the shoulder and stop. That is truly showing up.

Today, Sharon and I are honorary patrons of an effort—headed by Order of Canada member Mark Gillen—to plant 117,000 trees along the Highway of Heroes. Each tree will stand for a Canadian who died in service to Canada during overseas conflicts. For everyone—both at the repatriation ceremonies and

along the Highway of Heroes—these gestures are ways of showing our sorrow and respect for people who have undertaken those
responsibilities and suffered such tragic consequences. All these
people showing up in such a visible and genuine way build trust
in the service and sacrifice of our military. It also shows our
awareness of their role and our understanding of the sad and
awful consequences of war. If we are to build and maintain trust
in our military and in our country, those sad and awful consequences must never be far from our minds.

These consequences are never far from mine. Whenever I
attended repatriation ceremonies as governor general, I often
thought of a tour that Sharon and I, along with our friends
Debbie and David Beatty, made by bicycle through Normandy
and the twentieth-century battlefields of France. The most poi-
gnant memory for me was seeing the row upon row upon row of
headstones in the military graveyards. We were all overwhelmed
emotionally by seeing so many stark reminders of the terrible
tragedy of war. We noted that the headstones in one of the large
American graveyards were inscribed with standardized citations.
The smaller Canadian graveyard was different. Members of the
families had been invited to add their own personal descriptions
at the bottom of each headstone. I still remember one. It read:
"To the world, he was a soldier. To us, he was the world."

These words reinforce my belief in the value of showing up to
create solidarity and trust around a shared cause. The men and
women of Canada's armed forces showed up for us in the most
vivid sense imaginable. We all have a duty to show up and not
show off for them.

10

Act in the first-person plural

Putting we before me is the fastest way to build trust.

In my installation speech as governor general, I said Canada must be a smart and caring nation in which all Canadians can raise their talents to the maximum and use them to contribute to the success of the country. I went on to say that to become this smart and caring nation, Canadians must support families and children, reinforce learning and innovation, and encourage philanthropy and volunteerism. To encourage volunteerism, a first step we at Rideau Hall took after my installation was to revive the Governor General's Caring Canadian Award—which had been dormant for almost a decade due to budget constraints, and which we since elevated to become the Sovereign's Medal for Volunteers—to celebrate outstanding volunteers who give their time and talent to help others.

Undeniably, the most exuberant occasions on which we presented the medals were the We Day celebrations in cities across the country. The events bring together thousands of teenagers to hear and cheer a variety of speakers—young and young at heart—as they share their giving experiences and the knowledge they have gained about the importance of giving. These teens are selected for this daylong celebration due to their extraordinary volunteer efforts. These are not your usual gatherings. They are busy, loud, and full of excitement and enthusiasm—like 10,000 volts of electricity sending off sparks. Imagine 15,000 teenagers getting together in a rec room or backyard. The high-octane atmosphere of We Day achieves three goals. First, it celebrates the giving spirit of young people and, in doing so, encourages them and others to continue to give. Second, it brings young volunteers together to show them that they are part of something bigger than themselves alone. They are part of a giving movement that is changing the world. And third, it proves that volunteering is fun.

The National We Day celebrations stem from the Me to We social enterprise movement that Marc Kielburger and Craig Kielburger started in 2009. Their organization arranges international placements for young volunteers and supplies training programs and materials for young people who wish to improve their leadership skills. I was inspired to help Me to We after my first meeting with Craig. As a twelve-year-old in 1995, he established Free the Children, the forerunner of Me to We, to raise awareness about child labour in developing countries and help child labourers escape the violence and deprivation of their workplaces.

There is a story about Craig at age twelve appearing on the *Oprah Winfrey Show*. At the end of their televised discussion, Oprah said, "I am giving you $10 million to build schools in Africa," which was a total surprise to Craig. That evening in his hotel room, Craig got a call from Oprah's chief of staff asking for the name of Craig's communications director so the chief of staff could coordinate the announcement. Craig informed him that he did not have a communications director. The chief of staff replied that he would add another hundred thousand dollars so Craig could hire one.

I was drawn to Craig out of my amazement and admiration for someone so young who was not only giving but also energizing and mobilizing others to give. Joined by his brother, Marc, the Kielburgers' We Movement has grown to become the most powerful voice for caring young people that I have ever seen—or, more appropriately, heard. I was so impressed and inspired by it that I became the organization's patron shortly after I became governor general. Craig and Marc are also the youngest Canadians to be invested as members of the Order of Canada.

While Me to We is an impressive institution, moving from me to we—from the individual to the collective—is an even more potent way of behaving and communicating. I liken it to acting and speaking in the first-person plural. Behaving in this way arises from the universal human desire to achieve personal fulfillment by giving to others. Put simply, we give to others to complete ourselves.

A counterintuitive condition occurs when you move to the first-person plural: a large burden slips off your shoulders when your preoccupation is no longer yourself. When we become pre-occupied with improving the condition of others rather than the state of ourselves, we become less burdened by the tremendous loads we often take on in life—money, career, and personal advancement. I like to think the universe became a much more fascinating and attractive place for me when I realized I was not the most important person in it.

Speaking in the first-person plural—using the words "we" and "us" and "our"—is also an important way to move from the individual to the collective. It expresses empathy, encourages collective action, and shares credit. When combined, acting and speaking in the first-person plural is the fastest way to build trust.

As I mentioned earlier, one of the steps we took at Rideau Hall to underscore the connection between trust and happiness, and to endorse the importance of these qualities in creating a better country, was to revive the Caring Canadian Award. Governor General Roméo LeBlanc established this award more than two decades ago to recognize community volunteers and the work done by these unsung heroes. Informed by his own upbringing in a small Acadian village, he considered volunteers to be the glue that holds together towns across the country, as well as the many small communities that make up our larger cities. I agree. Volunteers are the unselfish people who live the Golden Rule every day. Without them, the quality of life for countless Canadians would be diminished. The Caring Canadian Award was a certificate granted by the governor general to volunteers. The ceremony would take place in the communities in which the volunteers in question did their good works. Sadly, the award lasted only a short time before falling victim to budget cuts.

When I became governor general in 2010, the award had not been given out for almost a decade. In my installation address, I identified philanthropy and volunteerism as one of three pillars in building a smart and caring country. So we set about to celebrate volunteering and volunteers in a formal way. We still did not have the money available at Rideau Hall to resuscitate the Caring Canadian Award, but we had just set up the Rideau Hall Foundation, one of whose functions is to find partners willing to contribute treasure and time for this and other worthy initiatives. The foundation not only raised the funds we required to revive the award, but also did so with a permanent endowment of $5 million that would bulletproof the award from any future budget cuts to the office. We set, and soon met, a goal of granting the Caring Canadian Award to 1,000 volunteers annually. (And if you think 1,000 per year is too many and may debase the award, I urge you to keep in mind that there are 40,000 official communities or "postal zones" across Canada, each of which has worthy volunteers, as well as many other people who can be encouraged to be such.) Within a few years, we proposed to Her Majesty the Queen that she elevate the Caring Canadian Award and rechristen it as the Sovereign's Medal for Volunteerism. Her Majesty was delighted with the suggestion and approved it promptly.

Of all the initiatives we undertook at Rideau Hall, this one is among the most meaningful to me. Our team travelled to dozens of communities to grant the award. We would gather with from five to fifty volunteers at city hall or some other important community centre and present citations to these caring Canadians. The presentation part of the ceremony would give us a chance to describe what each particular volunteer had been doing to support his or her community. These were modest yet powerful occasions. The volunteers were people of all ages and backgrounds who did what they did to make their communities better and the people in them happier. We recognized them not only because we believed what they were doing was important and should be celebrated, but especially because we wanted to encourage other people to follow their example. If we believe in a society where we look after each other, where we support each other in times of need, where we express our generosity daily, where the Golden Rule is an abiding presence, then we should applaud those who are showing us how these principles are actually being applied and encourage others to follow their lead. Invariably, the recipients would remark, "I really don't deserve this award. There are so many others in our community who not only enable me to help but also who do just as much." So very Canadian!

My biggest inspiration for acting and speaking in the first-person plural is my wife, Sharon, and our children. Our five daughters—Deborah, Alexandra, Sharon, Jenifer, and Sam—embody this spirit and have practised it since they were young. If We Day celebrations were held when they were teenagers, all five of them surely would have been there. Although our children grew up in an affluent family, they were acquainted early with people in need and tried to help fill that need by giving of their time. Their me-to-we thinking spurred them all to go abroad for several semesters and even years while pursuing their university degrees. This move set them apart from their peers and even from today's students. A mere 3 per cent of Canadian university students and 2 per cent of college students get any kind of international exposure.

Their experiences abroad sparked four qualities in them that I had observed developing in them during their teenage years. One, their natural curiosity as children was awakened further. Two, they became more tolerant—not merely tolerant that another person is different from them and that is okay, but an open-mindedness that welcomes differences. Remember Antoine de Saint-Exupéry's lovely observation: "You are different from me. But because you are different, you do not diminish me; you enrich me." Three, their judgement became better because they were able to look at most questions and situations from more than one perspective. (In fact, they regularly insisted on exercising this quality when their father was expressing an opinion!) They triangulated to solve questions, seeking out other sides of a story. They were very quick to spot ignorance or bigotry as a result. And four, they became more empathetic. They had the inclination and ability to walk in another person's shoes, and that empathy enabled them to develop a pluralistic outlook to their lives. They were able to hold two or more principles in their minds at once.

These four qualities made them more willing to trust and made them more worthy of trust from others. Our daughters are trusted because they have developed a positive response to differences, not a negative or neutral one. This response often leads to conversations that lead to understanding that leads to trust. As a result, very soon after meeting someone, they are able to find a commonality close to the heart or mind even though there may be differences on the surface or on the exterior.

Sharing examples of the Johnston daughters and young volunteers at We Day makes me fear I am giving the impression that acting and speaking in the first-person plural is the sole province of the very young. Walt Natynczyk's example shows that it is not. When I was governor general, Walt was kind enough to invite me to a gathering of his earliest army comrades to mark his retirement as chief of the defence staff from service in the Canadian Forces. Near the end of the party, Walt asked for quiet so he could say a few words. What stood out in his remarks most to me was his revelation that the biggest change in his professional life had not occurred when he was appointed chief of the defence staff—the highest uniformed position in the Canadian military. It came instead when he was promoted to lieutenant colonel at an unusually young age.

Walt said that he was excited about the achievement at the time because he had been striving for it ever since he was a teenager and realized he wanted to pursue a career in the military. He revealed that this moment of elation lasted for about one day. In a moment of profound insight, he discovered that, if he were to be a success in this new role, he would have to shift his focus. He must not revel in his personal achievement and concentrate his efforts on climbing even farther up the ranks. Instead, he determined he must devote himself fully to serving all the people in the regiment he had been assigned to lead. He must move from me to we.

Walt said that a great burden fell from his shoulders when he became aware that he was no longer going to centre his career on advancing himself. He likened the feeling to taking off a backpack full of battle equipment that an infantryman carries. It is the feeling of moving from the first-person singular to the first-person plural. Walt trusted in it. So should we all.

II

Be a barn-raiser

Neighbours who help each other with no expectation of immediate
return build more trusting communities.

When I was president of the University of Waterloo, my wife,
Sharon, ran a stable for thirty-six horses at our hundred-acre
farm in Mennonite country just north of town. The stable, known
as Chatterbox Farm, was a modest business that Sharon operated
more for pleasure than profit. Yet it was still a business, and businesses—especially those grounded in real property—require
insurance. One day, the insurance broker that Sharon dealt with
told her that the premium for the stable was scheduled to
increase. He suggested that he come by and make sure that she
had mitigated any safety hazards. That would help offset the
increased premium. He also pointed out that Sharon should

prepare a new estimate of the entire property's value. That way, she could be sure the policy was based on the most accurate value of the property. An overvalued property would inflate the insurance premium unnecessarily.

Made sense. So Sharon and the broker performed a safety audit of the property. Then some days later, Sharon herself went around the property with pen and paper in hand to determine the up-to-date value of the farm. While she was carefully examining the main barn, our Mennonite neighbour Edgar Schantz pulled up in his tractor.

"Can I help you with anything, Sharon?" he asked.

"Sure, you can tell me how much money you think it would cost me to replace this barn," she replied.

"What do you mean?" he said.

"I think $50,000 would cover the cost of replacing the barn, but I want to make sure my estimate is as accurate as possible," she said. "What do you think a replacement would cost?"

"Why do you have to put a price on it?" Edgar asked.

"If it burned down, I would have to know how much to claim in insurance," Sharon said.

"But, Sharon, if your barn burned down, we all would replace it for you," he said.

"What do you mean?"

"If your barn burned down, all your neighbours would help you," he said. "We would make sure the fire was well and truly out. The next day, we would gather and help remove all the rubbish left behind from the blaze. And then that coming weekend, we would again get together to build you a new barn."

"Really?" she said. "You would do all that for me?"

"Not just for you," Edgar said. "For any of our neighbours, we would supply all the manpower and materials necessary to build you a new barn—including the fastenings and the lumber, which we prepare at our mill."

Sharon was speechless for a moment as she contemplated what Edgar had just told her.

"Oh, wait," said Edgar. "I see the barn's roof is covered with asphalt shingles. We don't make those, so we would have to buy them. I guess we would have to buy about two thousand dollars' worth of asphalt shingles to cover a rebuilt barn of this size. So that would be the total cost of replacing your barn, Sharon. Two thousand dollars."

This conversation was Sharon's first direct encounter—and by extension, my own—with the time-honoured Mennonite practice of barn raising. This practice is a vivid example of the kind of behaviour that makes for a trusting community. Guided by the values of peace, community, and service, the Mennonites who make up the community north of Kitchener and Waterloo band together to help each other make it through hard times. When a neighbour's barn is destroyed by fire, extreme weather, or some other calamity, members of the community rally to raise a new barn. When a neighbour is felled by an illness for a lengthy period of time, members of the community till the field, harvest the crops, or do whatever other farm work is required until the neighbour is back on his feet. Whenever a neighbour is in need of any kind of support, even if that neighbour is not Mennonite, such as Sharon, members of the community supply whatever support the neighbour needs, with no expectation of immediate repayment.

When a spirit of barn raising exists in a community, the community is a trusting one and, as a result, a strong and resilient one: all community members trust in the knowledge—grounded in generations of experience—that they will step up to help a neighbour in need, and that their neighbours stand ready to help them if and when their time of need arrives. And just as barn-raisers give with no expectation of an immediate return, they also give according to their resources and skills. Preparing and serving a casserole at lunchtime during a barn raising is just as important to the effort as hauling lumber, constructing a truss, and hammering nails to secure shingles. Everyone helps raise the barn, but each gives toward the shared task in his or her own way according to his or her particular skill.

While the Mennonites' method of community self-reliance is founded on faith, it is one that neighbours in any community can emulate. Do you shovel your elderly neighbour's driveway after a snowstorm? If so, you are a barn-raiser. Do you take a turn flooding your neighbourhood's local rink? You are a barn-raiser. Do you coach a team in your community's baseball league or serve on the board of directors of your neighbourhood's community association? You are a barn-raiser. Do you do something, with no immediate expectation of return, to make your community stronger, more resilient, and more trusting? Then you are a barn-raiser. This fact may seem self-evident to some people. "Of course, I help my neighbours when they need it," these people might say. Yet even the most self-evident truths must be said out loud so that all may hear and know them.

Saying this truth out loud was at the heart of an initiative I was involved in at the University of Waterloo. I used to give a slide presentation titled "What's in the Water in Waterloo?" The first slide showed the beautiful Grand River flowing through the region. The second slide showed an overhead photo of a Mennonite barn raising. The third slide showed the second transposed over the first. Barn raising is in the water in Waterloo. Just before Sharon and I left to come to Ottawa in 2010, we helped create the Barn Raisers' Council, a group of community leaders who gathered regularly to focus on long-range projects to improve the health of the community. One I championed was the creation of a teaching hospital to accompany the satellite campus of McMaster University's medical facility, which came into the community and was affiliated with the University of Waterloo. The community also created an annual Barn Raiser Award to recognize the local leader who best exemplified the barn-raiser spirit.

Saying this truth out loud also was at the heart of My Giving Moment. Launched in 2013 by the Rideau Hall Foundation to encourage Canadians to build a better Canada by giving their time, talent, and treasure, My Giving Moment stressed how each of us can give because each of us has something worthwhile to share. Although the campaign stressed giving, we realized early on in the campaign that we should do more to emphasize the two-way nature of giving and receiving. Every giver needs a receiver. So we decided that we would use the campaign to feature "receiving" stories as well as "giving" stories.

I went first to break the ice. Pun intended. I shared a receiving story from when I was fourteen years old. It involved Mr. Taylor and a pair of skates. Mr. Taylor owned the sporting goods store near the one indoor arena in Sault Ste. Marie, my boyhood hometown in northern Ontario. He learned that a scout for a professional hockey team was coming to town to watch the team I was on play its next game, so he called me up at home and asked me to come down to his store right away. When I arrived, he told me that he had some new skates for me to wear for the game that night. These new skates were much better than the broken-down ones I was wearing at the time. In fact, apart from hockey sticks, I had never used or worn a new piece of athletic equipment. Equipped with the fresh pair, I could accelerate more quickly, stride faster, and deke more sharply than ever before. That combination of quicker, faster, and sharper must have worked. I scored a hat trick that night. I am still convinced it was the skates!

The thrill of my achievement lasted for a moment. What lasted much longer was my admiration for Mr. Taylor's gesture. Not only did I appreciate his deed, but I also wondered why this modest merchant would give me—a kid he really did not know—new skates so I could play better. He was not family. He was not even my coach. It made me ask myself: "Why did he do this thing for me? What did he have to gain from it? What did he expect in return for it?" I came to realize that he did it because he knew he had something meaningful to give someone. He did it because he knew even the smallest acts of giving matter. He did it because he knew that giving does not have to involve a grand campaign or be part of some reciprocal arrangement. He did it because he knew he was a member of a community that gave to help others, and he helped a young receiving kid realize the importance—and the joy—of giving.

When people give in this and similar ways, they build trust in their communities. This spirit of community trust can arise from such modest efforts as giving a lad a new pair of skates all the way to setting up a multi-million-dollar endowment that benefits an entire region. Arnold Witzig and Sima Sharifi are behind the endowment of which I speak. Arnold is an immigrant from Switzerland who came here in 2000 after he sold his logistics company; Sima is a refugee from Iran. Arnold chose Canada because he thinks the country is the most beautiful in the world. Sima found refuge in Canada around the same time after being jailed in Iran because she spoke out against the country's ruling regime. They met in Canada, fell in love here, and got married. They also fell in love with Canada's North—its geography, its special people, and its many cultures that arise from the conditions of the region. As a result of these twin love affairs, they wanted to see this special part of the world not only preserved but also to flourish even more—so much so that they endowed $60 million, their entire lifetime of assets, to create the Arctic Inspiration Prize.

Known as the Nobel Prize of the North, the Arctic Inspiration Prize is awarded annually at a grand gala. Money yielded from the endowment is invested in various projects designed to improve the lives of Northerners as defined by Northerners. The endowment, combined with contributions from Arctic Inspiration Prize partners, yields approximately $3 million a year, which typically breaks down into one $1 million prize, two $500,000 prizes, and a number of smaller prizes up to $100,000 that go to emerging projects led by young people. All projects are centred on the North and can cover an array of disciplines—culture, science, education, health, environment, poverty, and anything else that touches on and enhances the lives of Northerners.

Since the launch of the Arctic Inspiration Prize, Arnold has spent much of his time criss-crossing the North to build networks of support to make sure projects funded by the prize are sustainable beyond the prize money, to develop ambassadors for the prize in towns and villages across the region, and to stimulate overall interest in the prize and its works. An overarching characteristic of his travel throughout the North is to deflect attention from his and Sima's generosity and to shine a light on project leaders and the individuals and organizations that support projects. Arnold and Sima are splendidly selfless in this regard. They are barn-raisers.

Arnold and Sima entrusted the Rideau Hall Foundation with managing the prize. The foundation makes for a perfect partner—for two significant reasons. First, the foundation raises money to cover administration of the prize, meaning all funds generated by the endowment and partner contributions go to projects. And second, the foundation endeavours to ensure the most successful projects become ones that are sustained for many years, especially the initiatives that involve the health of Northerners.

My connection to the Arctic Inspiration Prize is also a personal one. Several months after I finished my tenure as governor general, Sharon and I were invited to dine with Arnold and Sima at their modest and cozy downtown Ottawa condominium. They were leaving in a few days to relocate permanently to their other home in Vancouver and would be driving cross-country in their 1989 Subaru. Arnold greeted us at the door wearing his usual apparel of blue jeans and turtleneck sweater. He also wore sealskin slippers and had an apron tied around his waist. He was cook for the night and prepared the most remarkable cheese fondue made of three cheeses blended beautifully and flavoured with kirsch, a brandy that is fermented from the juice of cherries. The recipe is from his home village in Switzerland. It was a delicious meal and an extraordinary evening. Sharon and I have enjoyed many grand feasts at Rideau Hall. Arnold and Sima's was on par with the best we ever had.

What was even more remarkable was that throughout the evening Arnold and Sima never talked about their generosity in creating this prize. Instead, they discussed their love for the North, their travels throughout the region, and their hope that the Arctic Inspiration Prize could help Northerners make substantial and sustainable improvements in their lives and, by extension, the life of the country. Sharon and I left that evening with a renewed belief in the remarkable nature of our country. Two people from extraordinarily different backgrounds chose Canada, found each other, and together are contributing all they have to make life better for a part of our country that is often overlooked by people in the southern part of the country.

Arnold and Sima are barn-raisers. They set up the Arctic Inspiration Prize as an expression of their desire to make a large community—a region and its people—healthier, more resilient, more prosperous, and more secure. So is Mr. Taylor, for wanting to help a neighbourhood boy raise his game. So is Edgar Schantz, who embodies the barn-raising ethos of giving with no expectation of return literally as well as figuratively.

So can we all. We can all be barn-raisers—not only for our immediate neighbours but also for our fellow citizens to help them make our country stronger, more resilient, and more trusting.

12

Know there is more than one right way

Pluralism enables people to remain united,
encourages them to work together, and engenders trust.

A favourite activity of mine while I served as president of the
University of Waterloo was to join the 150 or so in-residence students of Conrad Grebel University College for dinner. Affiliated
with the University of Waterloo, Conrad Grebel University College
is a faith-based liberal arts college founded by the Mennonite
church. Once or twice a year, I would go to the residence dining
hall, say a few words to the students, and answer some questions
from them. Then we would sit down and eat our meals together.
I really enjoyed these evenings. The students always welcomed me
warmly and asked insightful questions. And there is nothing more
invigorating than keeping company with young people.

One evening, a student came up to me after we had finished eating and asked whether she could ask me a difficult question. Sure, I said. She started by telling me that she was a new student at the college and was having a hard time. She said that she had arrived at the college with a fairly clear understanding of herself and her world, but that she was becoming confused about her identity and the kind of life she should lead as a result of all the new ideas to which she was being exposed. I asked her to give me an example. She replied that her faith as a Mennonite had led her to believe in a literal interpretation of the Bible, and what she was learning in her classroom discussions and through the books she was reading was eroding that faith. She went on to say that she was excited about the knowledge she was gaining but worried about losing what had been her rock for nearly all of her short life. She asked me what I thought she should do.

I responded by telling her that I was a lay reader in the Anglican Church and that my faith was important to me, too. I went on to say that what she was going through was healthy. It may not always feel that way, but it is natural for a young person who has chosen to leave her community and come to university to be exposed to a range of ideas and ways of thinking that challenge some of her cherished beliefs. I suggested that it was a good thing for her to test her beliefs and values.

Yet I also advised her not to discard quickly or completely the values that make her the person she is. The kind of self-inquiry she was experiencing was not an either-or situation or zero-sum game. She did not need to toss aside all she had come to know and replace it with something different. I told her that if you live long enough and stay curious you will find you will go through many similar bouts of examination and searching about yourself, the world around you, and how you fit into it all. It is good for you. It is healthy, even though it can get a little scary. The one thing to keep in mind as you go on your journey is this: there is no one right way to get where you are going.

To give her a little more comfort, I admitted that I encountered a somewhat similar situation when I left my hometown and started my first year at Harvard. It came while taking a course in the history of the United States taught by Donald Fleming, a famous and inspiring professor who taught at the university for forty-one years. The year before, at Sault Collegiate in my hometown, I had done very well in the provincial Grade 13 history course. We had one textbook for the course and I read it seven or eight times cover to cover. Yes, I have always been pretty keen about school. I do not have a photographic memory, but it is a good one, so for every question on a test or final exam—such as the causes and effects of Canadian Confederation—I could picture in my mind the three or four pages of text that related to it. I would then write out that information as quickly as possible. So when I received the provincial test scores, I was surprised to see that I had scored ninety-seven and I wondered what paragraph I had forgotten to remember! I was convinced I had faithfully replicated the information that I had absorbed from the textbook. That was how our knowledge of history was tested— reproduce that remembered textbook.

Fast-forward to Professor Fleming. We had no textbook for his class. He preferred original sources—speech transcripts, manifestoes, diary entries, and other documents created by people during the time period or events we were studying. Each week, we students had to complete six or seven readings that ranged from ten to a hundred pages. The first week went fine: it covered the introduction to the overall framework of the course. Not so much the second week. I read the six required documents and prepared index cards for each of the six, on which I summarized the main points and conclusion. After preparing the cards and comparing them, I realized to my consternation that the six documents came to six different conclusions or interpretations of the same question. I was confused. Which one was right?

So the next day, I went up to Professor Fleming at the end of class and said, "Sir, I have carefully read the assigned documents and each one comes to a different verdict about what we're studying. Which one is correct? Who is telling the truth?" He was probably wondering, "Where on earth did this student come from?" And he would have been right to say so. But he did not. Instead, the consummate teacher, he put his arm on my shoulder, looked me in the eye, and said quietly, "Maybe none of them." The light in my head went on. Just as the light in the Conrad Grebel University College student's eyes lit up in front of me. She smiled, thanked me, and then with a twinkle in her eye said, "That was very helpful, sir. I wish you had told us *that* during your remarks tonight instead of what you did tell us."

Knowing there is more than one right way is pluralism. In Canada, pluralism is a very old fact that continues to unfold. The Royal Proclamation in 1763 laid a formal basis for the treaty relationship between Indigenous and non-Indigenous peoples. That bargain recognized we must work together as different peoples if we are to survive and thrive in this vast and challenging land. It also led to several fundamental truths being enshrined in our country's laws and traditions: we are all here to stay; we are better off as partners; and pluralist thinking and acting is the most viable and perhaps the only path to lasting peace and prosperity in this place we call home. Knowing there is more than one way to get where we all want to go enables us to remain united, encourages us to work together, and engenders trust. Confederation is an exercise in pluralism, especially in the agreements and compromises made to make sure the so-called French fact in Canada was preserved and given the means to thrive. In fact, Canada is a social innovation—a society premised on the belief that diversity can work for us all and pluralism can produce creative harmony.

A modern example to us today is multiculturalism in Canada. In 1971, the federal government, following publication of the findings of the Royal Commission on Bilingualism and Biculturalism, adopted a policy of multiculturalism for the country. Eleven years later, this policy was entrenched in the constitution through section 27 of the Canadian Charter of Rights and Freedoms. Then in 1988, the Canadian Multiculturalism Act grounded this value further by recognizing Canada's multicultural heritage and committing the government to promote and protect it. Ours was one of the first two countries in the world to pass a multiculturalism act and, in doing so, to formally accept and encourage the influence of many cultures in shaping the evolution of a national culture. Why did we do that? If we went to the speeches in Hansard, I believe members of Parliament at the time said—perhaps not in these exact words—that we do so because this approach builds trust. Formally recognizing ours as a pluralistic, multicultural society says to people who bring a new voice to our country that they do not have to stifle that voice. It fits into the chorus of voices we have in this country. It gives that chorus a richer sound and produces sweet harmonies.

The Canadian Multiculturalism Act is an example of legislating trust. Canada enshrined in law the policy of multiculturalism as a way to reflect changes that were underway in the country and to influence more change in that direction. The act was a manifestation of change and a method to further that change. In doing both, the act strengthened trust, especially among new citizens. While the Canadian Multiculturalism Act is an excellent instance of knowing there is more than one way, it is just one example from our country's history. I raised section 27 of the Canadian Charter of Rights and Freedoms. Yet the entire Charter supplies a perfect illustration of a country not being bound by rigid thinking. Again, this approach does not emerge out of thin air. It is the product of many conscious decisions made over generations, such as the Royal Proclamation of 1763, Confederation in 1867, the Statute of Westminster in 1931 (which gave Canada its own voice in external affairs), the policy of multiculturalism in the 1970s, and the Charter of Rights and Freedoms in 1982.

One of my favourite examples of the understanding that there is more than one right way is the founding of McGill University.

Shortly before his death in 1813, James McGill drew up a will in which he left his summer estate and its land, along with 10,000 pounds, to the Royal Institution for the Advancement of Learning. The will stipulated that these resources must be used within ten years to set up a private college bearing McGill's name. McGill's heirs—his French Canadian widow and his stepson—initiated legal proceedings to contest the will, aided and abetted by officials of the Catholic Church in Lower Canada who objected to having a school—and a secular one at that—established beyond the purview of the Church.

Just before the ten years expired, all sides reached a compromise. The compromise was that McGill would not be bilingual, as James McGill had intended; it would not usurp the Catholic Church's then monopoly on education in French. The new McGill University would teach in English. McGill has evolved since that agreement to become one of the finest universities in the world. Yet a little-known custom, which dates back to McGill's beginning, is that students can write their exams or submit their essays in French if they are more comfortable in that language.

An illustration of the French language's standing at McGill University, and its resilience in spite of the compromise, is Wilfrid Laurier's valedictory speech to his graduating class in law in 1864—a class made up of thirteen students, divided almost equally between French-speaking and English-speaking students. It is the first public speech that this giant of Canadian life is believed to have made. Speaking in French, Laurier said that it matters not what altar we kneel at or what side we choose at the polling booth. Our differences are part of the compromise or the pluralism that defines Canada and makes it possible for our country to exist. It is only important, Laurier said, that we find a path forward together.

I tried to reflect this spirit as governor general when I presided over citizenship ceremonies. I would do so about once a year, before some fifty people of all ages who were becoming Canadian citizens. When I began each ceremony, I would say to those assembled: "Guess what? You are all bilingual today. We are going to recite the oath in French and English." Surprised (and occasionally worried) looks followed. I would then say each phrase of the oath in French, pause, and then have the new citizens repeat the phrase. And so on to the end of the oath. Then we would switch to English and repeat the process. When we were finished, they were Canadians.

What was most touching about the ceremonies was watching as some of the children helped their parents recite some of the trickier parts of the oath in one of the languages with which the parents were not so familiar. These open and eager children are living and breathing examples of pluralism—of knowing there is more than one way to reach a destination. What is most important, and what builds trust, is making sure we get to our destination together.

13

Tell everyone the plan

Successful teams are trusted to fully consider,
improve, and execute ideas and proposals.

Vimy Ridge holds special significance in the history of Canada and the minds of Canadians. It is a place of agonized conflict—the single deadliest and bloodiest day in Canadian military history. It is a symbol of determined courage, as men at arms from Canada achieved what their allies had failed to do for months at the cost of some 300,000 dead and wounded. And it is hallowed ground—"a patch of Canada" that is the final resting place of 3,600 men. To me, Vimy Ridge is all of these things. Yet this place and the battle waged here a century ago is also a lesson in the enduring value of trust.

The Canadians at the Battle of Vimy Ridge did several things differently than were done anywhere else during the war. The first was that all the Canadians in uniform were volunteers and not conscripts. They were there because they wanted to be there and had come to confront danger. Second, they were typically farm lads who had a bit of Canadian irreverence to them and—farm boys or not—had no sense of a class system. They had a little difficulty addressing their superior officers with all the proper deferential language and salutes. Though being attentive Canadians, they learned enough decorum to get by. Third, Canadian Major-General Arthur Currie and British Lieutenant-General Julian Byng, who was Currie's superior officer, did something that was completely different from the approach taken to that point by their British and French counterparts. They gave each soldier the battle plan. The British and French generals would never trust an ordinary private with the battle plan. Imagine their reaction: "Heavens, they're just privates. They wouldn't know what to do with the plan. They'd probably lose it in a bar or spill the beans, and the Germans would find it or get wind of it."

So every soldier was entrusted with a map of the battlefield and the details of the plan and the goal. Every one. And with these plans and at Currie's insistence, they then rehearsed rigorously for a month before the battle itself. That is a long time to have the plan in the hands of a bunch of ordinary privates. One of the consequences of this initiative was command succession in the heat of battle: when the sergeant of the platoon was killed or injured, the corporal stepped up and took his place. And when the corporal was sidelined, a private stepped up. The stakes were life and death.

A second major lesson from Vimy is this: no matter how much one tries to plan a battle, it becomes idiosyncratic; it defies the most detailed design the second the first shot is fired, and those in the fight have to adjust on the fly. Currie and Byng trusted the ordinary soldier to make the many appropriate adjustments, which they were in a position to make only because they had been entrusted with the entire plan. That is what Currie and Byng thought and practised, and that is one of their contributions to modern warfare. Again, Haig, commander of the British Army, and Pétain, his French equivalent, would not countenance that approach in the first three years of the war: "Inform ordinary privates with the battle plan and then practise it for days? Are you serious? Those people don't know what they're doing." Yet, thankfully, these Allied generals were at least open to the new approach developed by Currie and Byng. One has to think that, after spending several months and squandering many thousands of brave French and British lives in futility at Vimy, how could Haig, Pétain, and the rest of them not be?

There were other elements of the battle strategy in which Currie and Byng placed trust in their charges and changes—the science of battle, for instance. Andrew McNaughton of McGill University was a science advisor to the Canadian forces. (In the next world war, he commanded the 1st Canadian Infantry Division and then served as the country's minister of national defence.) He used airplane surveillance for the first time. The British and French did not trust this new machine in the air.

McNaughton also got hold of three young scientists from Cambridge University who were assigned to Haig's headquarters but who were not being used. These were bright and brainy young people. They worked to pinpoint—using sound and light distancing, which travel at different speeds—the positions of the German artillery and heavy guns. They also trusted in science through the use of sophisticated mathematics to design a creeping barrage—which was a revolutionary tactic at the time—that enabled the infantry to advance without undergoing the kind of deadly and destructive enemy fire they would have otherwise been forced to endure.

In earlier battles, artillery would bombard enemy lines through the night and then stop as the Allied soldiers began the attack at dawn. No further artillery was used so as to avoid killing one's own through "friendly fire." But when the infantry arrived, the enemy would have reassembled in their trenches. McNaughton's physics and mathematics produced a clockwork plan: an artillery barrage for five minutes followed immediately by an infantry advance of a kilometre, which would take ten minutes, and then halt. Artillery forces resumed raining shells one kilometre further for five minutes and then the infantry advanced another kilometre over ten minutes. Repeat the sequence endlessly throughout the day.

As many Canadians now know, these innovations, human and scientific—founded on and fuelled by trust—resulted in triumph for the Canadian Corps at Vimy Ridge. Currie became leader of the Corps soon after the victory—the first time a complete army marched under a Canadian's command. He and his troops honed and applied their approach over the next year and a half to great success. So much so that the Canadians became recognized as the "shock troops" trusted to take on the most difficult assign-ments in the forthcoming battles.

Then it stopped. Following the war, Canadians and others—
inside the military and beyond—largely reverted to traditional
hierarchical methods. Why did the trust-based approach of
Currie and the Canadians fail to take hold? The particulars
and immediacy of the wartime situation had much to do with
it. Thousands were being killed and maimed. No progress was
being made. Like I said, the stakes were literally life and death.
In those conditions, novel methods were more likely to be
accepted. With these conditions gone, however, everyone fell
back on previous ways. In fact, the industrial and managerial
economy of the twentieth century was solidifying according
to practices that dominated organizational behaviour for the
next eighty years—personnel segmented according to strict
hierarchical layers, and tasks isolated to specific individuals or
groups. These rigid divisions of responsibility and labour on
the factory floor and in the office building held sway for gen-erations. Leaders came up with ideas and plans; the rank and
file carried them out.

It has taken nearly a century but that approach has given
way to the one employed by the Canadians at Vimy. In what
might best be called the New Organization, ideas are not
judged based on who came up with them, but on whether they
work. And to come up with workable ideas, all personnel of the
New Organization must be informed of and come to own its
direction and goals. In a nod to the men at Vimy, they must
know the full plan.

I witnessed a vivid illustration of the advance of the New Organization when Malcolm Gladwell—the best-selling author of *The New Yorker* fame who popularized ideas such as the tipping point and the 10,000-hour rule—gave a convocation address at the University of Waterloo in 2007. His father is a lovely guy—a distinguished retired professor of civil engineering who taught at Waterloo for many years. I was then the university's president and we wanted to engage Malcolm, who grew up in the city of Waterloo, went to the high school there, and then went off to accomplish great things. So we named him literary advisor to our Faculty of Arts. We also awarded him an honorary degree and he gave a splendid convocation speech. It was very brief—only five minutes long—and he delivered it extemporaneously.

Gladwell spoke to graduates about how organizations have changed, about how some organizations function well and not well, and about the emergence of the New Organization. He told a story about CAE International, a Montreal company that designs, develops, and sells some 70 per cent of the flight simulators now in use throughout the world, and is now the largest trainer of pilots. Gladwell told us of his experience being at the company's facility to watch a flight simulation for a pilot and co-pilot. They were to respond to a simulated malfunction and subsequent loss of one engine on take-off of a twin-engine narrow-bodied aircraft with 150 people on board. They had to get the damaged and underpowered plane up in the air, away from the runway to dump the plane's fuel, and then land safely back on the runway. Gladwell recalled that it was a half-hour exercise, at the end of which his shirt was soaked with sweat because he was so engrossed in what the participants in the simulation were doing.

After Gladwell plucked his soaking shirt away from his skin, he said he realized that what he had just seen revealed three lessons about modern organizations. Lesson one is the clear and impressive display of how the human brain works to extract large amounts of information from many different sources and processes that information to make specific decisions to deal with certain situations. You had the pilot in the left seat and the co-pilot in the right. You had a huge number of gauges, dials, and sensors surrounding them. Each of the two was using the maximum of their cognitive capacity to look at much data and choose the most pertinent, move that data to information, and then crystallize it to knowledge. That is how the New Organization thinks.

Lesson two is the seamless communication back and forth in succinct bursts between the two professionals. One has information that the other needs, and it is fed from that person to the other right away. And the communication goes back and forth seamlessly. That is how the New Organization communicates.

Lesson three is the absence of hierarchy, ego, or entitlement. The co-pilot must have the confidence to override the pilot when the co-pilot has better information. The pilot must be willing and eager to get that new information and accede to its priority, knowing it will enable them both to make a better decision. That is how the New Organization acts—built on trust.

These three lessons are not evident in the old organization but are much in evidence in the new. Together, they make up what is a fascinating trust relationship—the cognitive capacity to absorb and synthesize vast amounts of data, convert some of it into useful information, and then translate it into immediately applicable knowledge; the ability to communicate very quickly, usually using short code words and not full sentences; and the willingness, even eagerness, of a superior to take and act on information supplied by a subordinate, and that same eagerness of the subordinate to supply the information.

This kind of trust relationship is the essence of the New Organization. We saw this organization on display in April 1917. We see it much more today. We will see it everywhere tomorrow.

14

Depend on those around you

Top leaders trust in the knowledge and talents of others.

My favourite definition of leadership is recognizing your total dependence on the people around you. I realize this notion of dependence might sound trite at first—like I am just recommending that leaders thrust themselves into situations where they inherit a parade of talented people, then jump in front of that parade and presto—you are a great leader! Not quite. What makes this principle worth following is this: leaders are responsible for the careers of the people within their organizations, and the primary job of leaders is to make sure those they lead can function right up to the limit of their talents.

I have found that when people are in organizations in which they are empowered to reach the limits of their talents, they usually find their own ways to push out these boundaries farther because they are excited about what they are doing and how they are growing. They discover talent they did not realize they had. That performance, expansion, and excitement is a natural consequence of a leader placing his or her trust in their followers and, in doing so, creating a working environment in which it is exciting and rewarding for them to work and, ultimately, successful for everyone.

I am not exactly sure when and in what circumstances I discovered the wisdom of recognizing that leaders are wholly dependent on those around them. It may have dawned on me subconsciously when I was the teenaged coach of some very young athletes. I came to understand fairly quickly that my success as a coach and our success as a team were dependent not on my brilliance as a tactician or as a dressing-room motivator but on my trusting in the abilities of others and making sure they were in positions in which they could exercise those particular abilities to the fullest extent.

Think of a successful football team. It is made up of many players who function in a variety of specialized positions that rely on distinct abilities—running, passing, catching, blocking, tackling, kicking. The overall team's success is based on trust that flows from the coach and spreads throughout the team. Without it, the team is destined to fail, or at least fall well short of fulfilling its potential.

Or think of the conductor of a symphony orchestra. Conductors are powerless in the sense that, of all the members of the orchestra, they have no ability to make a sound. A conductor

is "instrumentless." But such is the connection between a conductor and as many as a hundred musicians that they create a
beautiful harmony. What power of persuasion and trust!

I truly became aware of this kind of trust when I began managing universities—first as principal of McGill University and
then as president of the University of Waterloo. I characterize
this time—from 1979 to 1994 and then from 1999 to 2010—as
being years in which the cause and the company were very good.
So I was lucky. Yet I still realized I was completely dependent on
the people who make up these organizations. In fact, because of
their unique hierarchy, universities are an excellent case study in
the value of recognizing your dependence on those around you.

The top layer of an institution of higher learning is the executive team. The next management layer in this setting is the
Deans' Council, which tends to be the most important group in
the administration of a university. Each dean is responsible for a
faculty, which has its own life. (As an aside: if you lead a university, you better have the confidence and trust of the deans. If you
do not, things go downhill fast.) Then you get into the schools,
departments, institutes, individual professors, staff, and students.

Let me focus on the professors. A professor's loyalty is first to
their individual disciplines or sub-disciplines. Their next loyalty
is to their immediate colleagues and students, usually within
their respective departments, and then to their faculties or
schools—be it arts, engineering, law, and so on. Last of all, their
loyalty is to the university. Frankly, that is not a hierarchy through
which, at first glance, to build trust. Universities do not work well
when individual faculty and staff members have little sense of

loyalty to and trust in the overall cause. If you are a professor, researcher, or administrator whose only trust relationship is with your immediate discipline—you are a brilliant biochemist, say, dealing with organic chemistry—if that is your only world, the university could go to hell in a handbasket and you would not really care, at least immediately. You would likely have many other places and opportunities open to you.

So how does a leader build trust in a setting that has such a definite and sometimes rigid hierarchy? To start, the circle around you has to be porous, so that you can let into that circle and interact with as many people and as many different kinds of people as possible. I put this thinking into action with the senior executive teams that I led. Typically, I would never have more than five people reporting directly to me. I did not want to build a sort of palace guard meant to serve only me. In fact, I wanted to decentralize the executive team as much as possible. This approach enables people throughout the organization to get a clear sense that it is not the office of the president that is running everything in the institution—rather, each person has a say in the decisions of the institution and can help steer it in a direction on which they agree. This approach produces a reciprocal trust. When leaders show they trust others in very real ways, those others usually express the same quality in return. It flows both ways to create a trust relationship.

Leaders can make this decentralization more pronounced and the trust relationship stronger by moving budget authority down to the faculty and department levels, and not restricting this function to head office. At Waterloo, we devoted less than

130
—

5 per cent of the annual operating budget to "central administration." The mean figure for all Ontario universities was
approximately 15 per cent. The rest went mostly to the deans
and department chairs.

On the flip side, the leaders at one university I know created
an office of the president that was a bit like an inner corporation.
The office was made up of a small circle of people that cut itself
off from the rest of the school. It soon became an embattled circle
of wagons like those you might recall from watching old Westerns
on television. If you are president or part of a small group of vice-
presidents of any organization, you want to be circulating and
visible throughout the organization as much as possible.

To maintain this circulation and visibility, I made sure I
served as a professor as well as president. As McGill University's
principal—that university's equivalent to president—I continued to teach in the law faculty and to research and write books
and articles for scholarly journals. At the University of Waterloo,
we did not have a law faculty, so I did not teach very much, but
I continued to write. So I was a professor, doing professorial
things and, therefore, I was able to build and maintain a trust
relationship with other faculty members—both by interacting
and engaging with these professors and by these professors
seeing me carrying out this role. Yet I was also the executive in
chief of the entire university.

It kept me busy, but it paid off. I remember being at a meeting
of the selection committee for my renewal for a second term at
Waterloo; there were one or two cynical people on the committee who I sensed wanted to catch me up short. One of them said,

"You know, this is a place of scholarship and yet most of our administrators are not scholars. Have you written any books?"

This person had been at the school for some thirty years. I replied that I had written some books. He asked me how many. I said, "Twenty-one and I'm currently working on the twenty-second." He then asked me how long I had been a university administrator. I said that I had been one for about twenty-seven years, which I always regarded as being on partial administrative leave from being a full-time professor.

I mention this conversation because any leader does not want to have two classes of citizens in their organization. While the staff of a university supports the faculty in many respects, a leader does not want to put the faculty in a position where it can say truthfully, "We are the real university doing the research and the teaching, and then you have some small circle of executives, supported by large bureaucracies called the staff, getting paid a lot of money that could be put to better use in classrooms and labs."

The same thinking applies to any organization. The leader of the institution can forestall that kind of argument by not building up a sort of Imperial Guard around himself or herself. This layer is designed to protect the time of the grand poohbah, because that guard believes the most precious time the leader can spend is in the company of the guard. That is a corrosive environment for any leader in any organization to create. In fact, both at Waterloo and McGill, all our vice-presidents (save administration, finance, and external relations) and deans continued to teach and pursue scholarly activities while being administrators.

I tried to follow a one-class approach when I arrived at Rideau Hall in 2010. When we brought in new talent, we made sure they were made part of the permanent staff and not exempt staff whose tenure would coincide with my own. In this way, we wanted to create a staff whose loyalty was to the institution and not to the individual in office—be it me or anyone else. Partly as a result of this organizational approach and, of greater importance, as a result of the quality and commitment of the staff of the institution, the people who worked at Rideau Hall flourished. As I mentioned earlier, in 2016 Rideau Hall was named the top employer in the public sector of the National Capital Region. When we learned the happy news, Stephen Wallace—who as secretary to the governor general was primarily responsible for creating this structure and leading the team—and I sent around a note to each of the 150 staff of the office. The note pointed out that the Organisation for Economic Co-operation and Development had just finished its annual survey of the quality and professionalism of public services within its thirty-three member countries and Canada was named number one. The note continued: "Please bear in mind that this office—your office—of the Government of Canada has just been recognized as the top employer in the region. That combination of achievements should—we trust—make you all feel pretty good about the work you are doing on behalf of Canadians. You are the top of the top, the best of the best."

This approach was not the only example of our efforts to nurture trust at Rideau Hall. On my second day as governor general, I received a thick bundle of dossiers. Each one contained not only a letter for me to sign, but also a summary sheet bearing as many as seven different sets of initials of the many people who had researched, drafted, formatted, fact-checked, proofread, revised, and approved the letter for my signature. This process—one drafter and six checkers—troubled me greatly. So we changed things immediately. Instead of following an approach that scattered responsibility so widely that it evaporated, we instituted a "one-over-one" method. The first "one" is the individual who took on the lion's share of the work to produce the document. The other "one" was my signature. And given the number of documents I signed each year, I was not much of a fact-checker. This approach gave the first "one" a direct sense of responsibility and, with it, pride and satisfaction in his or her work. It also was a respectful use of people's time and energy. Of course, if the writer encountered a drafting difficulty, they were encouraged to seek advice—and they did.

This combination of responsibility and respect was trust made real, and it produced a reciprocal trust—or trust relationship. We took advantage of this reciprocal trust to institute a delivery standard of one-day turnaround for letter in and reply out—a tough standard but one we believed we could and did meet because of the trust relationship we built up through the one-over-one method. We applied the philosophy on approximately 40,000 documents signed annually. This number jumped to 100,000 during 2012 when Rideau Hall handled 60,000 Diamond Jubilee certificates, all of which I signed with my own hand because I believed in making some form of tangible personal contact whenever possible in this digital age.

Although these achievements at Rideau Hall are noteworthy, this chapter would be woefully incomplete were it not to include the person on whom I was most dependent during my time as governor general, and throughout my married life of fifty-four years—my wife, Sharon. Both Sharon and I recognized right from the moment I was offered the position that I could succeed in it only if we approached it as a truly joint endeavour. We turned out to be right, as Sharon played both her own singular role and a complementary role with me at Rideau Hall gatherings, on our many visits throughout Canada, and on our foreign missions.

On the foreign missions we led—where personal diplomacy with heads of state and senior officials of government is so fundamental—Sharon's influence and impact were evident right from the start of my tenure, and even before, since the first foreign trip we were advised to take occurred prior to my October 1, 2018, swearing-in as governor general. I risk breaking the convention of nondisclosure about official meetings with members of the Royal Family by relating the story of this trip, but I will trespass a bit because of the unique personalities involved. Sharon and I were lucky to be asked to present our credentials to Queen Elizabeth one weekend in August, when Her Majesty and the Duke of Edinburgh were at their Scottish castle, Balmoral. Sharon and I took with us every type of formal clothing one could possibly imagine, but we never put a stitch of the fancy gear on. Balmoral is an eighty-thousand-acre estate secured around its perimeter, but the Queen goes to great lengths to make life at the residence as informal as possible.

A case in point: at breakfast on Saturday morning, Her Majesty and Sharon were discussing their plan to spend some time at the stable with the horses. Nothing could please Sharon more—and Her Majesty—than to spend a Saturday morning with horses. But she quickly realized Sharon lacked proper stable shoes. So Queen Elizabeth jumped up from her chair at the table and went upstairs to her bedroom. When she returned, she had in her hands a pair of well-worn but sturdy brogues. Passing the shoes to Sharon, Her Majesty said, "There you go, my dear. We have similar sized feet." And Sharon wore the Queen's shoes for the entire weekend.

Another example of Sharon's influence was her quick rapport with the Duke of Edinburgh. The Duke is noted for having a wry and sometimes even a wicked sense of humour, which matched Sharon's wit perfectly. Proof of their complementarity was evident as we drove around the Highland paths of the estate. The Duke drove one Land Rover with Sharon as passenger, while the Queen drove another Land Rover with me as passenger. Even though we were in a separate vehicle, I swear Her Majesty and I could hear the bursts of laughter emanating regularly from the other Land Rover. At one point, they were laughing so hard I was quite certain the Duke was going to lose complete control of their vehicle and drive it off the road. Without Sharon, I likely would have survived the weekend without making any diplomatic gaffes, but it would also have been a much less successful and certainly a much less fun journey.

Sharon was just as warm and engaging with some of the most vulnerable people on the planet. Our grandchildren cherish a video they have of Sharon in Botswana visiting a hospice for children with AIDS. She regularly would have her own itinerary of events during our visits outside and inside Canada. While at the hospice, Sharon frolicked with and embraced the children as if they were her own grandchildren. The highlight of the video for our grandchildren is the sequence in which their grandmother leads a group of happy revellers in dancing the limbo—not only dancing, but also doing so while wearing a short, tight skirt and demonstrating her athleticism by gyrating in perfect rhythm under a very low bar. Their grandfather was more restrained in his enthusiasm.

At home, Sharon was no different. She often enlivened our formal ceremonies at Rideau Hall just by being herself. At one Order of Canada investiture dinner, the happy chatter, laughter, and shouts of joy coming from her table were so clear that I got up from my table and went over to make sure a bun fight was not about to break out. Not to worry, said one of the guests, who told me she never would have thought in her wildest dreams that a formal event at Rideau Hall could be such fun.

That was Sharon's influence in a nutshell: she made everything we did at Rideau Hall—even the more serious and sombre occasions—worth taking part in. Two events stand out in my memory, both of which she organized in partnership with Bell Let's Talk, the Bell Canada program to promote mental health education, research, and awareness. The first was the showing of *The Maze*, a film on the life of Ukrainian-Canadian artist William Kurelek. Named after the celebrated painting of his own brain, the film depicts the demons Kurelek struggled with in his efforts to regain his mental health through art and religion. A copy of the painting hangs in Sharon's office.

Not only is the film a powerful artistic achievement worthy of being seen in its own right, but also having it screened at Rideau Hall was a visible testament to Sharon's work to bring mental illness out of the shadows and into the light. Her efforts go back years to her early professional days as a physiotherapist and occupational therapist working with mentally ill children. In this role, Sharon was a champion for bringing modern approaches to the treatment of mental illness.

The second and sequel event was The Masquerade, an outdoor concert on the grounds at Rideau Hall. Everyone at the gathering wore masks and, at the appointed time in the concert, took them off. This act was a metaphoric way to confront the darkness of mental health, bring it into the open, and begin to move down the path to cure and rehabilitation. Again, this event, as well as the many speeches she gave and visits she made to mental health organizations, exemplified Sharon's efforts to remove the public stigma associated with mental illness and help increase and improve research of treatments and cures.

Further proof of Sharon's influence and efforts was the fact that the Navy named her the honorary captain of the military unit responsible for military personnel and their families. In this role, she travelled widely across the country to meet men and women who served in the armed forces, many of whom were experiencing post-traumatic stress disorder and other physical and mental ailments as a result of their service in the military. She also made a point of making personal connections with the children of these service members, as they were often going through their own pains as a consequence of a parent's illness. At these gatherings, the rapport that Sharon had with all assembled was palpable and was largely due not only to her knowledge about mental health but also the natural empathy and humility she showed in abundance.

These examples merely scratch the surface of Sharon's activities and leadership while we were at Rideau Hall. She was so busy and involved that she would often say to me that she viewed our five-year mandate in office as a marathon made up of stages or milestones. It was the best way for her to pace herself so that she could complete the busy and lengthy task. But then my tenure was extended for a further two years. And that was a stretch. When we stepped down on October 2, 2017, it took Sharon about six months to recover her physical health and equilibrium. As proof of her happy recovery, I note that as I am finishing this manuscript on Easter weekend of 2018, she has returned from her routine of rising at six a.m. or so, writing for the morning, riding her horse at noon, and then getting on with the rest of her day. She is midway through writing her second novel in a trilogy that began with *Matrons and Madams*, which is about her grand-mother. The second novel is about her mother and the third is about us, which terrifies me. All royalties from the books have gone and will continue to go to the mental health research fund she has started at the Royal Ottawa Hospital.

Sharon has been the wind beneath my wings almost continu-ously since I was her first date in high school at age thirteen, and she has performed her own vivid arcs of flight in the sky. My dependence on her only increased during our time at Rideau Hall. Any success we may have achieved in those seven years was possible only because of her. There is no one I trust more.

Part 3

Create a trustworthy and trusted country

Six ways to think and act that will strengthen trust in your country's public institutions and international reputation

---

15

Recognize a present peril

Dramatic changes in how people communicate and share information weaken their trust in institutions and in each other—at least temporarily.

The revolution in information and communications the world is going through now is not unprecedented. The historical parallel that is keenest in my mind goes back hundreds of years and involves three men—John, Martin, and Fred.

John is Johannes Gutenberg. Around 1450, he came up with the first printing press in Europe. An earth-shaking development, you say? Not quite. The people who were able to read—a minority of the overall population to be sure—were still willing to pay for manuscripts that monks would write out by hand. As a result, John soon went bankrupt, religious texts in Latin being the only documents people back then deemed worth publishing and reading.

To realize the revolutionary promise of John's machine took the initiative of our story's second character—Martin. Around 1525, seventy-five years after John went bankrupt, Martin Luther translated the Bible from Hebrew and ancient Greek into German, so that people who could read German could gain access to the word of God for themselves.

Yet it took still another man to enable Martin to fully realize his ambition. Enter Fred. Known formally as Frederick the Elector of Saxony, he sheltered Martin from unforgiving Catholic grandees in Rome, making it possible for the radical scribe to accomplish his task; it was Martin's German-language Bible that, years later, was translated into English under the auspices of King James, yet another protector.

At this point in our story, John's technological revolution re-enters the picture—even though he had by then been dead for many decades. The versions of the Bible translated into German, English, and several other languages were finally produced in large quantities, so they could be placed in the hands of what became, slowly but surely, an ever-increasing audience of readers.

The combined effort of John, Martin, and Fred constitute a transformation in how human beings communicate. Although it took several hundred years to occur, the information and communications revolution spurred by these three men changed the world in two meaningful ways.

By making it possible for people to share ideas much more rapidly and cheaply than ever before, the printing press took Europe out of the Dark Ages (from 500 to 1100) and Middle

Ages (from 1100 to 1453) and into the light of the Reformation and Renaissance. These movements then propelled future generations of Europeans along new avenues of social, economic, and artistic development. It is easy to overlook that, prior to John, Martin, and Fred's revolt in information and communications, Europe was a backward civilization when contrasted with China, India, and the Muslim world. The Dark Ages were the long night of the European mind.

The changes incited by John, Martin, and Fred also bring to my mind a word we are hearing more of these days—disintermediation. Back in their day, the most important relationship that an ordinary person had, especially if that person were a serf, was their relationship with God. But that relationship was made possible only through intermediaries of stone (the awe-inspiring cathedrals and other structures of the Catholic Church) and of flesh (the priests, bishops, cardinals, and popes who purported to be the only messengers authorized to deliver the word of God). These earthly go-betweens presented themselves as the sole means through which ordinary people could worship, gain salvation, and one day enter God's eternal kingdom—as opposed to that, ahem, other place down below.

The awe that these structures and officials inspired was a core ingredient in faith. John, Martin, and Fred's revolution undermined the authority of these religious way stations and middlemen by putting the word of the Bible onto the printed page that the masses could access by themselves and into languages that the masses could assess for themselves. This vital combination of accessibility and "assessibility" began the prospect of self-learning, or learning without any intermediation by the ecclesiastical authority or hierarchy; that was the beginning of the disinterme-

146
—

diation of religion and the slow wearing away of the Church's monopoly on imparting God's truth.

The transformative influence of John, Martin, and Fred is not news to me alone, nor is it something we in the twenty-first century can perceive in hindsight only. There is a remarkable passage in Victor Hugo's novel *The Hunchback of Notre Dame*— published in 1831 and set in 1482—that captures the migration of power from that book's titular church of stone and glass to the seemingly humble page. It involves the novel's main antagonist, Claude Frollo, archdeacon of Notre Dame Cathedral. Hugo writes:

> The archdeacon gazed at the gigantic edifice for some time in silence, then extending his right hand, with a sigh, towards the printed book which lay open on the table, and his left towards Notre Dame, and turning a sad glance from the book to the church—"Alas," he said, "this will kill that."

The book will kill the cathedral. The page of ink is more powerful than the edifice of stone. Such is the strength of disintermediation.

This passage by Victor Hugo neatly summarizes the influence that John, Martin, and Fred had on organized religion. Yet it is a mistake to restrict the revolution's influence to religion. If we imagine freethinking and self-learning as a stone dropped into a pond, the ripples flowing from that dropped stone are the end of serfdom, which led to the mass migration of people to

Europe's cities, which led to the Industrial Revolution, which led to the notion of the right to education, which led to the rise of democratic governments and the world we know today. Ripple by ripple.

This journey was not completed overnight, of course. It took some three hundred years for the printed word to reach a majority of the population of Western Europe. By the time it did, the old authorities either were gone or weakened dramatically and were replaced by literate publics and democratic governments.

We gain at least three lessons from the information and communications revolution spurred by the combined effort of John, Martin, and Fred. The first is that when we make it possible for people to enjoy greater degrees of self-learning, not merely is faith re-examined but also all received knowledge is susceptible and even likely to undergo reappraisal.

The second is that this kind of upheaval tends to play out much more quickly and extensively over time. The communications and information revolution of the printed word brought on by John, Martin, and Fred took some three centuries to reach all of Europe. Today's digital communications and information revolution has been much faster, more widespread, and dynamic. It took the Internet a mere decade—from 1995 to 2005—to reach a majority of the world's population, placing in the palms of their hands all the world's knowledge. The pace, extent, and complexity of this change increases seemingly daily—as the computing power of modern machines becomes much stronger; as these machines and their software gather, manage, and evaluate ever-growing masses of data; and as advances and applications of artificial intelligence and virtual reality become more sophisticated and relevant.

The third lesson is that these changes throw into confusion and then replace traditional sources of facts and truth. In the era of John, Martin, and Fred, the guardian of truth was the Church, and it fought hard to keep its authority and monopoly on the truth. Umberto Eco's 1980 novel *The Name of the Rose* is an excellent depiction of the Church's desperate efforts to maintain control of what it considered the truth.

We see all three lessons at work in today's information and communications revolution: received knowledge is undergoing reappraisal; the ways in which we take in and spread that knowledge are happening faster than ever before; and traditional sources of truth are being challenged and overturned as a consequence. While our constantly connected life today is exciting, this existence is full of risks as well as delights. Just as the established authorities in the times of John, Martin, and Fred learned, the primary risk concerns trust in each other, in our public institutions, and in media old and new.

In Canada, we see this phenomenon playing out before our very eyes. In 2016, the Edelman Trust Barometer measured our country's trust in media at 55, which is neutral. That figure dropped dramatically to 45 a year later, placing Canada, for the first time since Edelman—a communications marketing agency—has been conducting its trust research, among the "distruster" countries when it comes to the media. The 2018 score for Canada is 49, which puts our country in the distruster camp, just one point ahead of the global average. I should add that Edelman's surveys in other Western countries, notably the United States, United Kingdom, and France, show significantly different and more dramatic depar- tures from traditional sources of trust.

Digging deeper into Edelman's findings, we confront some conflicting numbers. On the one hand, 65 per cent of Canadians worry about false information or fake news being used as a weapon. This concern has led us to become less trusting of search engines and social media and more trusting of traditional media. Especially noteworthy, the credibility of journalists has increased substantially.

On the other hand, majorities of these same people believe news organizations are primarily concerned with attracting big audiences; are willing to sacrifice accuracy to be first to break a big story; and are more beholden to advancing an ideological position than to informing the public honestly. As a consequence, a majority of Canadians are disengaged from news altogether, consuming news less than weekly. Edelman reveals that, instead of conventional news sources, increasing numbers of Canadians consider business leaders to be the country's most authoritative voices.

So let me get this straight: our trust of journalists is rebounding, yet we are exposing ourselves less and less to what these trusted sources are telling us; our trust of traditional media is leaving our trust of social media in the dust, yet we suspect traditional sources are more concerned with inflaming audiences than informing them; our trust in business leaders is growing, yet we do not seem to have come to grips with the consequences this development will have on democracy in Canada. Is having CEOs replace journalists and public officials as truth-tellers and trust-builders a healthy sign or an indicator of just how far the once trusted have fallen?

Results from the Canada-centric research carried out by Proof Inc. are not as troubling as those presented by Edelman. According to the Proof CanTrust Index for 2018, trust in the news media remains steady: 51 per cent of respondents indicate that they trusted the news media; the figure for 2017 was 50 per cent. One notable finding by Proof, however, mirrors that of the Edelman study: many Canadians have moved their trust from new media back to traditional media. As evidence, Proof finds that the Canadian Broadcasting Corporation/Radio Canada is highly trusted by Canadians (at 73 per cent), while trust in Facebook dropped significantly (from 51 per cent to 34). I suspect this result stems in large part from the role Facebook played in disseminating untrustworthy news during the 2016 U.S. presidential election campaign.

Alike at times and dissimilar at others, the Edelman and Proof results reveal to me just how fluid trust is at the moment and is likely to remain for the foreseeable future. Not only is this fluidity evident in our media, it is being influenced by how new media cause us to think and behave. New methods of communicating and sharing information do not on their own cause the divisions that erode trust. These divisions have always been there and are in some respects healthy. What these new media have done is amplify and harden divisions. Different sides do not merely interpret facts differently, but they also see and spread different facts. Different people with different facts undermine our rule of law, which lies at the heart of our democracy. If we as a country have difficulty agreeing on what we consider real or the truth, how can we arrive at the answers, let alone the compromises, necessary to do anything to improve?

Just as troubling, new media seem to be designed expressly to arouse feelings before people have time to ascertain the truth. This fact leads to an undermining of trust in most things and, sooner or later, in the very source of the information, and, of course, these same communications tools hold open to some the ability to mislead deliberately, to spread falsehoods and lies quickly, to create chaos and undermine trust widely. Adversaries need no longer attack each other physically. They favour assaults on the trust their rivals have in their neighbours and shared institutions. They achieve their ends by spreading half-truths and untruths, preying on a population's inability to distinguish between fact and fiction.

Not surprisingly, we all have roles to play in stabilizing and restoring trust in how we communicate and share information. Individuals can stabilize and restore trust by being as truthful as possible in what information they create and share, and by being as responsible as possible in how they use that information. Each of us also faces the challenge of becoming more literate digitally, so we can be more discerning in judging, sharing, and commenting on the information we come across and that is pushed into our various news feeds.

Media professionals can stabilize and restore trust by avoiding cynicism, believing in right and wrong, and upholding the highest professionals ethics. They can build trust further by steering clear of circulating rumours published by others, by making sharper distinctions between commenting and reporting, and by requiring owners, editors, and maybe even journalists to declare financial and other interests and thereby avoid any real and perceived conflicts of interest. In short, they can act professionally.

Professionals at two of Canada's biggest newspapers are showing the way in this country. The *Toronto Star* and the *Globe and Mail* have launched initiatives to rebuild trust with readers of their newspapers, websites and apps. Known as the Trust Project, the *Star*'s effort centres on what it calls an interdepartmental trust committee that looks "into how the *Star* can foster greater reader trust and develop journalistic and technological tools to bridge the trust and media literacy gap." The Toronto paper also is publishing a growing list of stories to draw back the curtain on its operations to give readers a closer and clearer look at how important everyday decisions are made at the *Star*. The stories range from how the newspaper's critics go about their jobs, to how the paper decides to publish breaking news, to how the *Star*'s editorial board operates.

The *Globe and Mail*'s initiative, also known as The Trust Project (but with an uppercase letter in its article), places the longstanding Canadian newspaper in a consortium of media outlets around the world that have adopted a group of trust standards and protocols. According to the *Globe and Mail*, these standards and protocols are not only transparent ownership and mission statements, and ethics and reporting policies, but also clear labelling of story types and links to detailed author information. The idea behind these machine-readable standardized indicators is that they will help readers, search engines and social media sites identify journalism that is worthy of trust.

Leaders of search engines, social media sites and other new media devices and platforms can learn from these two trust projects. More precisely, they can stabilize and restore trust by taking action against those who use the latest communications tools to create chaos. Taking my cue from the work of the *Toronto Star* and the *Globe and Mail*, I suggest the next step in the evolution of these communications technologies should be adopting current and creating new advances that enable us to make judgements about the trustworthiness of information and information sources. How these functions would work I leave to others, but if we can assess the creditworthiness of borrowers and assess the reliability of vendors on Amazon, sellers on eBay, and service providers on Uber, then surely we can do more to assess the trustworthiness of information and its sources. Our communications revolution has improved the accessibility of information and communication to unprecedented levels—just as John, Martin, and Fred's revolution did in their time. The time has come to improve its "assessibility" as well.

Public institutions can stabilize and restore trust by showing they value the solid, valid information that makes it possible for our democracy not only to operate properly but also to survive. We tried when I was governor general to show the office's high regard for accuracy, honesty, and integrity in research and reporting by hosting gatherings at Rideau Hall for many awards, honours, and distinctions that relate to communications and information. These gatherings covered a variety of truth-tellers and trust-builders—such as teachers, journalists, historians, and scientific researchers. We made a special effort to expand this group by inviting the three main research-funding agencies of the federal government—the Social Sciences and Humanities Research Council, Natural Sciences and Engineering Research Council, and Canadian Institutes of Health Research—to hold their many award ceremonies at Rideau Hall.

Schools at all levels can stabilize and restore trust by ensuring young people have the curiosity and ability to distinguish between evidence that is valid and evidence that is not, and then to use that discerning judgement when making decisions and taking actions. This discerning ability and inclination will lead them to insist that their public institutions be open and speak the truth, rather than seek to hide or obfuscate through cant, exaggeration, and myth.

To equip young people with this curiosity and discerning eye, our schools need to make some dramatic changes in the way they teach. To start, we need to really begin taking advantage of what we know about how the mind learns and thinks. We have come to understand more in the last twenty-five years about how the human brain functions than we knew in the previous three thousand years. Yet we are still teaching in ways we did decades ago. Too often, students are just copying down what their teachers tell them, rather than thinking about ideas and methods, then critiquing them and applying them in different contexts. Today's all-too-familiar and all-too-common method may have been excusable before, when teachers were the source of all knowledge simply because they had read many more books than students had. Yet students nowadays have so much more information at their disposal. Certainly more than any one person can teach in a classroom. As a result, the job of the teacher should be more Socratic—not providing data but joining with students in a curiosity-sparking journey from data to information to knowledge to wisdom. Today's teacher helps students form the questions, not supply the answers.

When it comes to Canada, we also should make it possible for many more young people to be exposed to the globe. That means studying all kinds of maps, learning second and third languages, and, later in their academic lives, studying, volunteering, or working abroad for a least a semester, especially in a language other than their own. As mentioned in an earlier chapter, only 3 per cent of Canadian university students and 2 per cent of Canadian college students go abroad for any period of time for an academic exchange or volunteer assignment. We have to open up the world physically, as well as virtually, to help young people gain the comparative experiences necessary to distinguish between truth and lies, between facts and falsehoods, between reality and myths.

An excellent example to expand upon is the Queen Elizabeth Scholars program. Founded in 2012 to mark the Queen's Diamond Jubilee, this partnership among the Rideau Hall Foundation, Universities Canada, and Community Foundations of Canada has already enabled some three thousand young doctoral, post-doctoral, and early-career researchers from other

countries to come to Canada for graduate studies, and young
undergraduate and graduate students from Canada to travel
abroad for four to twelve months for internships and academic
exchanges or to work on development projects in Commonwealth
nations throughout the world. I hope this program will become
a permanent legacy to Queen Elizabeth when she finishes her
remarkable tenure as sovereign.

Carrying out any of these recommendations—let alone all of
them—will not be easy and will not be done overnight. I am also
aware of how tenuous any suggestions I make are in light of the
rapid and dramatic changes that no doubt lie ahead. Facebook,
Google, Apple, Amazon, and others are shaping our world in
many ways—some of which are no doubt unclear. Many of us
have placed our trust in new communications technologies and
the companies that create them. An entire generation knows of
no other world than their hybrid on-line/off-line worlds. For
many of this generation, their on-line worlds are more intricate
and intimate than their "real" worlds. How does this fact influence trust? Are people abandoning the conventional civic world
of voting, going to community meetings, and visiting their
neighbours for virtual worlds? It appears so. Is the result of this
migration a weakening of trust in conventional manifestations of
community? Again, it appears so. Are we in a sort of no man's
land between old mechanisms of trust—the conventional sources
of information and insight such as newspapers, community
meetings, election campaigns—and new manifestations of trust
that are glimpsed but yet to be realized? Is blockchain technology
or a derivative of it the future of trust?

Many questions. Not nearly as many answers. The only true answer we have is that dramatic changes in how people communicate and share information weaken trust—at least temporarily. Our challenge is not only to harness the benefits but equally to recognize and address the undermining of trust in our continuously connected lives.

Don't believe me? Just ask John or Martin or Fred.

16

Invite others to dance

Trust grows when diversity becomes inclusion.

Diversity is not enough. It is not enough for Canadian businesses, organizations, and institutions to have written policies or mission statements that proclaim, "We are committed to being a diverse organization, and we will have recruiting and hiring policies that enable us to be diverse." While the wide-ranging backgrounds and experiences of Canadians is a strength and advantage when we compare our country to others, diversity on its own is at best a missed opportunity and at worst a mere facade. Our businesses, organizations, and institutions need to go beyond an approach that tabulates differences according to demographic traits, ethnic origins, and socio-economic identities to one that unites us by taking advantage of our diversity. The goal is to move from diversity, a fact, to inclusiveness, a process and action. Trust is built when our workplaces move from having a diversity of faces to having the people behind these faces included meaningfully in making decisions and taking actions. Trust is built, as my colleagues at Deloitte say, when we invite people to dance and not when we invite them merely to the dance.

Dancing is not just a metaphor. As governor general, I met every individual ambassador—typically, fifty or more a year—when each presented his or her letter of credence. The team at Rideau Hall tried to be as systematic as possible in how we welcomed new ambassadors. We would do our best to receive an ambassador no more than thirty days after he or she arrived in Ottawa. Often sooner, because representatives to our country cannot function with the necessary authority until their letters of credence have been received officially. We organized at least one ceremony each month, with as many as half a dozen new representatives to Canada. The ceremonies were formal and dignified, as they should be. Yet we also tried to balance the occasions by making them warm, friendly, and personal. After the official part of the function, I would meet each ambassador one on one for ten minutes or more to learn something about his or her family, professional background, and specific goals for their time in office. I would then supply whatever advice I could to help them move a little closer to achieving their goals and to adjust to life in Ottawa.

Part of that adjustment advice was to encourage them to attend the annual Rideau Hall winter party for the diplomatic community in the city. It was the one social occasion of the year in which we had all ambassadors and high commissioners in Ottawa together in one place at one time for a classic Canadian winter fête. The centrepiece of the occasion was the Rideau Hall skating rink, which now functions for five months of the year thanks to a donated refrigeration plant that keeps the ice the right temperature. These diplomats, some from countries in which snow never falls, would be out on the ice learning to skate, with instructors from the Minto Skating Club there to help. And they enjoyed every minute of it—together. If enough snow were on the ground, we also had a horse-drawn sleigh to bear groups of diplomats around the grounds at Rideau Hall. Snowshoes and cross-country skis also were at the ready.

Then we would move indoors and join a group of fiddlers from Maniwaki, Quebec, a small town located about a two-hour drive north of Ottawa. The fiddlers not only played their instruments and sang (in French and English), but "called" and taught the diplomats how to square dance. So this diverse group of "new Canadians" were dancing together in harmony. The fiddlers turned some guests into performers by teaching them how to play the spoons and join in on the singing. They even went so far as to instruct the newcomers in the gymnastics of square dancing. In so doing, this group of diplomats—representing a wide range of cultures—were not passive observers of Canadian cultural customs. They took active—indeed, exuberant—roles in creating the entire experience. They were contributing to it, influencing it, owning it.

That is what I mean by going from merely inviting a diverse group of people into an organization to having that group included meaningfully in the decisions and actions of the organization. That is what I mean by inviting people to dance and not merely inviting them to the dance.

Another way of understanding the move from diversity to inclusion is to look at it as a progression from optics (a surface diversity of backgrounds and experiences) to outcomes (drawing on the knowledge and talent that stems from these diverse backgrounds and experiences to improve the performance of an organization) to ownership (using that greater performance to expand diversity, deepen inclusion, and empower everyone even further). When an organization shows that it trusts all the members of a diverse team and believes that each member has something worthwhile to contribute, that team responds by making a contribution greater than it otherwise would have made. This is ownership. The greater performance that ownership produces is tangible: more innovation, greater employee retention, and increased profitability. All of which makes employees, executives, and shareholders happy.

This kind of ownership of inclusiveness is what a business, organization, or institution should want to achieve. Commissioning a report from an esteemed consultant or an internal team and then issuing a well-intentioned mission statement is one thing. The much better thing is to cultivate an organizational culture in which everyone understands what true inclusion is and uses this understanding to enhance their own work and the performance of the organization. Organizations should not want merely to invite people to the dance. They should make every effort to get people out on the dance floor, engaged in a common activity and using that activity to build trust.

If I may be permitted to extend my metaphor (as well as the diplomats' Canadian winter party) a little further, the best dance is a square dance, because people are dancing as a group and not as individuals or as couples. In a square dance, each person is part of a group that must work as a unified whole. If the group is really successful, it also sings the tune together. And if one couple bumps into another, which happens with considerable frequency for newcomers to a square dance, then everyone has a good laugh. Which brings them even closer together.

We can take this idea of ownership and broaden it to cover countries and regions. In their book *Why Nations Fail*, economist Daron Acemoglu of the Massachusetts Institute of Technology and economist and political scientist James Robinson of Harvard University show that inclusion underlies all successful countries. Their basic premise is that those societies that are inclusive in their economics and politics thrive. Those that are extractive fail. Teasing out their thesis a bit more, successful societies are those whose economies create incentives, reward innovation, and permit everyone to participate. These inclusive economies are sustained by equally inclusive political institutions that are accountable and responsive to citizens and that distribute power broadly so as to constrain the arbitrary or capricious exercise of it. On the flip side, extractive political institutions concentrate power in a narrow elite and place few constraints on this elite's exercise of power. Their economics and politics are extractive. Economies in these societies are usually structured to extract wealth from their natural, capital, and human resources for the benefit of the politically powerful elite. These economies remove incentives, stifle innovation, and dissuade participation.

The dichotomy of inclusion and extraction was the subject of a long conversation I had with German chancellor Angela Merkel when she came to Canada on a state visit in 2015. She stayed at Rideau Hall and we arranged to talk at length in the company of five or so accompanying German ministers. Our conversation was not one of niceties and platitudes that these meetings can be on occasion. Ours was a respectful and polite discussion, but it was also quite direct. The quality of the conversation was due in large part to Chancellor Merkel's curiosity and intelligence. She was a research chemist early in her career and the daughter of a Lutheran pastor. Her English is also excellent. Much, much better than my German. I was cross-examining her on the state—and especially the fate—of the European Union. I consider it a remarkable institution that shows how people from many backgrounds and experiences can prosper and live in peace when they make room for diversity and inclusiveness. It was no surprise to me that the EU won the 2012 Nobel Peace Prize. Among my questions were: What factors are doing the most to weaken Europeans' trust in the EU? What are European leaders who believe in the EU doing to address these factors and bolster trust in the union? What can these leaders do to counter the efforts of those who seek to undermine trust in the EU?

Chancellor Merkel then put the burden on me, challenging me to explain—in detail and with examples—how Canada has managed to make its crazy quilt of a country work so well for so long. She was amazed that the many powerful centrifugal forces within our country—language, region, race, and religion—had not caused Canada to scatter into a thousand pieces.

I responded first by giving her a copy of *Why Nations Fail*—I had bought a dozen or so copies for just such occasions—and proudly explained the book was a product of the Canadian Institute for Advanced Research, or CIFAR—an especially apt acronym when you soften the "C." I then expanded on the thesis of *Why Nations Fail*, underscoring the dichotomy between inclusive and extractive countries and suggesting that Canada's largely inclusive politics and economics had created a national atmosphere of trust that helped Canadians of all regions, languages, and interests to curb their passions and check their disputes. A mutual trust, which has been built and strengthened over generations, has given us the resilience to weather many political and economic storms without resorting to the level and persistence of violence that has torn other peoples and nations apart irrevocably. We are a nation of evolution and not revolution. This trust has been tested and even stretched to the breaking point several times in our history: the trial and execution of Louis Riel, the conscription crises during both the first and second world wars, and at points during the sovereignty movement in Quebec. Chancellor Merkel paused at one point during our talk to ponder the word "extractive." Then, for several minutes, she went back and forth in German with her five ministerial colleagues about the meaning of the word. They ended up compiling seventeen synonyms for extractive. Given the intensity of their dialogue, I was confident I had made my point.

While Acemoglu and Robinson do an excellent job and service with their book, *Why Nations Fail* is not the first time I encountered their thesis. One encounter came decades ago courtesy of James Michener, one of my favourite authors, whose observations of history I have found most compelling. He authored more than fifty books, and I believe I have read every one—some more than once. In his nonfiction book on Spain, he begins with the central question, How did Spain, the leading European power in the fifteenth century, fall to mid-power status and insularity by the eighteenth century? He explores this question region by region in his literary journey through Spain.

Finally, around page 500, Michener arrives at the University of Salamanca and states that at last he has found the answer to his question. In 1492, while King Ferdinand and Queen Isabella were sending Christopher Columbus to America, the Inquisition did its greatest damage at the University of Salamanca. It was the jewel of European centres of learning. Kings and dukes sent their scholars first to Salamanca before Oxford or Paris for solutions to their most complex questions. But here the Inquisition of the Catholic Church began a systematic dismantling of Spanish scholars. First, the Moors—the Islamic professors—were banned from the university and then from Spain; then the Jewish teachers were cast out; then the scholars in science and medicine; and finally any teacher who challenged religious orthodoxy was dismissed. So comprehensive was this intellectual and scholastic shedding that by the eighteenth century the famous University of Salamanca was little more than a finishing school for highbred young Spanish men to teach them manners; Spain turned its back on diversity of thought and the commerce of ideas from Europe and the East and became mesmerized with plundering Latin America.

What I learned from Michener, as well as from Acemoglu and Robinson, from Merkel, and from diplomatic parties and exchanges at Rideau Hall is that when we take advantage of diversity and use it to become inclusive—in other words, when we invite people to dance and not merely to the dance—we build trust.

17

Apologize

Expressing regret is a necessary first step on
a long journey to restore trust.

No book on trust, certainly no book on trust written by a
Canadian today, would be proper or complete without addressing
our country's failure to earn and keep the trust of Indigenous
peoples in Canada. The litany of broken promises, the countless
half measures, and the scores of false starts are too numerous for
me to recount here. Overshadowing them all are the colonial and
often downright racist attitudes held by generations of people in
our country. Ours is a shameful history in this regard and it is our
responsibility to face up to that truth.

The Truth and Reconciliation Commission was an honest and
earnest effort by Canadians to confront reality and, in doing so,

halt the erosion of trust between the country and Indigenous peoples in Canada and begin the long journey of restoring trust.

A product of the Indian Residential Schools Settlement Agreement, the commission was created first to gather the facts about the residential schools in Canada. Developed and administered by the Government of Canada and Anglican, Catholic, Presbyterian, and United churches, the schools were used as tools of assimilation. More than 150,000 children attended residential schools scattered across the country; some 80,000 of these students are still alive. Many of these children suffered physical and sexual abuse. All of them experienced some form of enduring traumatic pain that stemmed from being separated from their families, communities and cultures, sometimes forever.

Along with establishing the truth about the residential schools, the commission had a duty to assess the legacy of these schools and their treatment of students; recommend ways to heal the consequences of that treatment; and outline steps that Canadians and their government should take to restore trust between the government and Indigenous peoples in this country. While these steps are vital, a step taken even earlier was essential. That earlier step—the one that began the entire process—was an apology.

In the 2008 apology to the eighty thousand living former students and all family members and communities of these students, Prime Minister Stephen Harper said in the House of Commons:

The government recognizes that the absence of an apology has been an impediment to healing and reconciliation. Therefore, on behalf of the Government of Canada and all Canadians, I stand before you, in this Chamber so central to our life as a country, to apologize to Aboriginal peoples for Canada's role in the Indian Residential Schools system.

To the approximately 80,000 living former students, and all family members and communities, the Government of Canada now recognizes that it was wrong to forcibly remove children from their homes and we apologize for having done this. We now recognize that it was wrong to separate children from rich and vibrant cultures and traditions and that it created a void in many lives and communities, and we apologize for having done this. We now recognize that, in separating children from their families, we undermined the ability of many to adequately parent their own children and sowed the seeds for generations to follow, and we apologize for having done this. We now recognize that, far too often, these institutions gave rise to abuse or neglect and were inadequately controlled, and we apologize for failing to protect you. Not only did you suffer these abuses as children but, as you became parents, you were powerless to protect your own children from suffering the same experience, and for this we are sorry.

The burden of this experience has been on your shoulders for far too long. The burden is properly ours as a Government, and as a country. There is no place in Canada for the attitudes that inspired the Indian Residential Schools system to ever prevail again. You have been working on recovering from this experience for a long time and in a very real sense, we are now joining you on this journey. The Government of Canada

sincerely apologizes and asks the forgiveness of the Aboriginal
peoples of this country for failing them so profoundly.

Nous le regrettons. We are sorry. Nimitataynan.
Niminchinowesamin. Mamiattugut.

Prime Minister Harper's direct and unequivocal apology was a
necessary first step to rebuild trust, because no progress can be
made to redress and overcome past wrongs without the perpetra-
tor of these wrongs holding itself to account. His successor,
Prime Minister Justin Trudeau, has continued and broadened
this expression of regret by making clear the colonialism that is
inherent in Canada's history. Prime Minister Trudeau spoke at
length about this truth in front of the world when he addressed
the United Nations General Assembly in 2017. He said:

Canada is built on the ancestral land of Indigenous Peoples—
but regrettably, it's also a country that came into being without
the meaningful participation of those who were there first. And
even where treaties had been formed to provide a foundation
for proper relations, they have not been fully honoured or
implemented.

For First Nations, Métis Nation and Inuit peoples in
Canada, those early colonial relationships were not about
strength through diversity, or a celebration of our differences.
For Indigenous Peoples in Canada, the experience was mostly
one of humiliation, neglect, and abuse—of a government that
didn't respect their traditions and strengths, or their distinct
governments and laws, but instead denied and undermined

their rights and their dignity. That sought to overwrite their distinct histories, to eradicate their distinct languages and cultures, and to impose colonial traditions and ways of life. That discarded the Indigenous imperative to protect the land and water, of always thinking seven generations ahead.

In doing so, we rejected the very notion that whole generations of Indigenous Peoples have the right to define for themselves what a decent life might be. And we robbed Canada of the contributions these generations would have made to growing our great country.

The failure of successive Canadian governments to respect the rights of Indigenous Peoples in Canada is our great shame. And for many Indigenous Peoples, this lack of respect for their rights persists to this day. There are, today, children living on reserves in Canada who cannot safely drink, or bathe in, or even play in the water that comes out of their taps. There are Indigenous parents who say goodnight to their children, and have to cross their fingers in the hopes that their kids won't run away, or take their own lives in the night.

Young Indigenous people in Canada struggle to get a good education. And though residential schools are thankfully a thing of the past, too many Indigenous youth are still sent away, far from their families, just to get the basic education most Canadians take for granted. And for far too many Indigenous women, life in Canada includes threats of violence so frequent and severe that Amnesty International has called it "a human rights crisis."

That is the legacy of colonialism in Canada—of a

paternalistic Indian Act; of the forced relocation of Inuit and First Nations communities, and a systematic denial of Métis

rights and history; of residential schools that separated children as young as five years old from their families, punished them for speaking their own language, and sought to extinguish Indigenous cultures entirely.

Having these truths uttered by our country's prime minister is unprecedented in our history. Yet having the prime minister and other leaders state hard truths and express genuine regret and shame is the necessary first step toward reconciliation and the restoration of trust. Hearing the voices of those who have suffered is also essential to this process. These voices—uttered by First Nations, Inuit, and Métis organizations and individuals—have expressed the support of Indigenous peoples in this country for reconciliation. They have also rightly stated that reconciliation will be a long and difficult journey—perhaps an unending one—that will require the active and ongoing involvement of all Canadians and all public institutions in Canada as we move closer to recognition, respect, justice and harmony.

We must heed their words. We must also recognize how the forceful statements made by prime ministers Harper and Trudeau underscore the different roles played by elected government officials and the governor general in our country, and how these roles are fulfilled on undertakings such as reconciliation. The federal government carries out what Walter Bagehot termed the efficient role in the Westminster parliamentary system. This role oversees the daily operations of government through public policies and money. The counterpart to the efficient is the dignified. This role performs the ceremonial aspects of government.

For this set of dual institutions to work properly requires trust between officials on both sides of this efficient-dignified equation. The prime minister—on the efficient side—and the governor general—on the dignified side—must understand where the dividing line between the two institutions exists and must make sure their activities and decisions do not stray across that line. So even though the relationship between the Crown and First Nations peoples in Canada dates back centuries to the time when European settlers first arrived on the continent in substantial numbers, the governor general nowadays is in no position to govern this relationship. Our constitutional traditions, as well as our laws, have evolved significantly since then.

This fact was brought into relief in the lead-up to the Crown–First Nations Gathering on January 24, 2012. The 170 First Nations chiefs who were to attend the meeting were adamant that I as governor general be present to receive them and deal with them directly as the representative of the Crown in Canada. Officials in the Prime Minister's Office and we at Rideau Hall were quite firm in maintaining that First Nations representatives could not negotiate over policy with the governor general. What I chose to do in that situation was convey the message and petition along to the prime minister and minister of Indigenous affairs as a matter of courtesy. My decision reflects the separation that must exist between elected and unelected officials in our democracy. Yet the separation does not mean that the governor general, as representative in Canada of the country's head of state, has no role to play on important public matters such as reconciliation between the Government of Canada and Indigenous peoples in the country. For example, when I served as governor general I fulfilled the vital dignified function of the office by serving as honorary witness before a gathering held in Edmonton of the Truth and Reconciliation Commission for the survivors of Canada's Indian residential schools. My wife, Sharon, was honoured to serve as honorary witness in Ottawa when we hosted the final meeting of the Commission at Rideau Hall.

As a result of our service as witnesses, we have a responsibility to survivors and through them to all First Nations, Inuit, and Métis. The duty of the witness in Indigenous cultures is three-fold. First, witnesses must observe keenly what they see. Second, witnesses must listen carefully to what they hear. And third, witnesses must share widely what they see and hear, so that other people may understand what has happened and act on that understanding. In other words, they must be trusted messengers and ambassadors.

Recognizing this truth, we at Rideau Hall—both in the Office of the Governor General and in the Rideau Hall Foundation—took several actions to contribute to the much larger effort of achieving reconciliation between Canadians and the country's First Nations people. Some of these actions built on initiatives that had begun much earlier in my tenure.

The Truth and Reconciliation Commission recommended two in particular. The first action was to hold information sessions on reconciliation for employees of the Office of the Governor General. I encourage all departments and agencies in the federal public service to follow this straightforward move if they have not done so already. The second action was to use the annual gatherings of the governor general, the lieutenant governors of the ten provinces, and the commissioners of the three territories—which we call the vice-regal family—to carry out joint initiatives related to reconciliation. To direct these initiatives, we established a Crown–First Nations task force co-chaired by the lieutenant governors of Ontario and British Columbia. One of the decisions made by the group was to create special celebrations in Ottawa and in regional capitals on National Aboriginal Day each June 21. During these mixed-honours ceremonies, members of the vice-regal family conferred a variety of territorial, provincial, and national awards to a group of some fifty Aboriginal and non-Aboriginal Canadians who had made significant contributions to reconciliation.

The activity takes advantage of the role of these vice-regal offices to confer honours on worthy Canadians. It also built on our effort at Rideau Hall to take some of our honours ceremonies on the road and not hold them in Ottawa exclusively. Its purpose was very simple: to cast a positive light on some of the inspiring people and their actions to advance reconciliation substantially across the country. To add to the excitement and magnitude of the events, we invited past honourees who lived in the particular regions to attend. Like the people being honoured, these past honourees represented a range of awards, including the Order of Canada.

A third action we took while I was governor general was to identify an aspect of reconciliation and then use the convening power of the office of the governor general to advance that specific component. Working through the Rideau Hall Foundation, we chose education—in particular, successful completion of secondary education by First Nations, Inuit, and Métis students and moving on to post-secondary school. Fortunately, the Mastercard Foundation was eager to get involved with crucial funding. Its $22.5 million investment in the Rideau Hall Foundation, as managing partner, to support innovative programs at Yukon College and Vancouver Island University is helping Indigenous students make successful transitions to college and university.

The successful transition to universities and colleges for First Nations, Inuit, and Métis students in Canada is fraught with barriers. One main obstacle among many is the fact that many Indigenous students are older than typical students and have young children. Leaving the support of their communities to attend college and university can place enormous financial, emotional, and family pressures on these students. These programs supply the specialized backing these students need to make their transitions smoother and their post-secondary education more likely to end in graduation.

Enlisting First Nations, Inuit, and Métis people as co-creators of the programs has been the key ingredient in their success. The Rideau Hall Foundation bases all its Indigenous programs on the principle of "nothing about us without us." Indigenous leaders at Yukon College have remarked that their involvement in creating the program was the first time that anyone had asked them what they needed. Their experience to that point involved outsiders coming into their communities, schools, and homes and telling them what was needed. This co-creation approach builds trust, makes it more likely that programs will achieve their goals, and moves us all closer to achieving reconciliation.

I want to reiterate that all these actions were undertaken in the wake of Prime Minister Harper taking that critical first step and apologizing to surviving students of Indian residential schools and through them to all First Nations, Inuit, and Métis people in Canada. It is a lesson we should all remember when seeking to restore trust in our personal, business, and civic lives. Without first admitting that we have committed a wrong act and apologizing clearly and unequivocally for it, we cannot hope to carry out the journey to restore the trust we have broken.

I was reminded of the scope and sanctity of our country's journey to reconciliation with First Nations, Inuit, and Métis people when a group of chiefs presented me with a drum at Rideau Hall. Perry Bellegarde, who is now national chief of the Assembly of First Nations, asked me to accept the drum and to ensure it would remain silent until the day when reconciliation has been achieved and trust recovered between Indigenous and non-Indigenous people in Canada. When that day comes, National Chief Bellegarde said to me, he and his fellow chiefs— or their successors—would return to Rideau Hall and let the drum speak.

The drum today rests in a place of honour at Rideau Hall, ready for the day when the chiefs return to hear what the drum has to say—their signal that trust has been restored to their satisfaction. Regularly during my tenure as governor general, when I gave people a tour of the building, I would point to the drum, highlight its significance and make a wish that the day will soon come when Canadians will hear that drum and the songs it brings. Our guests were always stirred emotionally by the drum, as I am. It bears silent witness to our willingness and, ultimately, to our success or failure as Canadians to face up to the truth of our history and then carry out the long journey to reconciliation—a journey that began with a humble yet essential apology.

18

Honour our teachers

Applauding those who exhibit widely cherished values builds trust.

At one point in my installation address as governor general, I said, "If you remember only three words from what I say to you today, they are 'cherish our teachers.'" I spoke this phrase because I wanted my audience to revere the people who have imparted to them and continue to impart the most valuable lessons in life. Each of us has had a teacher or teachers whom we have turned to once or regularly for wisdom, encouragement, and inspiration. Our teachers might be that literally—teachers in classrooms, laboratories, and lecture halls. Just as likely, they are parents and grandparents; aunts and uncles; neighbours and friends; coaches and bosses; teammates, classmates, and colleagues; and mentors who counsel personally and role models we have never met, yet whose examples motivate us daily. During the speech, I continued by saying that if we had a whole day together, I could share at least a hundred stories of teachers in the classroom and outside the classroom who have influenced me throughout my life.

Although the kind of teacher I have relied on has changed over time and under different circumstances, the constant quality my teachers have possessed is a particular value or set of values that I admired and wished to adhere to in my own life. They taught not only through their words but more so through their examples. For instance, Purdy Crawford, my mentor as a lawyer, taught me fairness—that everyone deserves the chance to rise as high as their smarts and energies can take them. Miss Wilkinson, my Grade 10 English teacher, taught me empathy— that reading about the lives of others exposes us to different perspectives, widens our own experiences, and deepens our understanding of other people. And my colleagues at the United Way in Montreal taught me humility—that just because you have reached a privileged position in your city does not mean you know all that is going on in your city. The older I get, the more I come to understand that the example one gives or sees is the most important teacher of all. Yes, a wise bit of advice or friendly word of encouragement can do wonders at critical times, but we heed that advice and gain confidence from those encouraging words because we trust the character of the teacher who supplies them.

Examples of trustworthy teachers abound. There is Clara Hughes. An Officer of the Order of Canada, member of Canada's

Sports Hall of Fame, and one of our country's most dedicated and decorated athletes, Clara went on a 12,000-kilometre, 110-day cycling journey in 2014 to speak with Canadians about mental illness and, in doing so, reduce the stigma associated with these illnesses. During Clara's Big Ride, she travelled through every province and territory, visiting 95 communities and 80 schools, and attending more than 260 public events. At these events, she told her story about dealing with mental illness and, in doing so, instil hope in others and bring mental health farther out of the shadows. At one of the final stops of her incredible journey, I presented Clara with the Meritorious Service Cross (Civilian Division) to recognize her actions in bringing great benefit and honour to Canada. She is a teacher.

There is Chris Hadfield. An Officer of the Order of Canada, Commander Hadfield is one of the world's most accomplished astronauts. In 2013, shortly after Chris concluded 146 days in space in command of the International Space Station, I awarded him the Meritorious Service Cross (Civilian Division), making him the first person to hold both the civil and military decorations of this honour. He is a teacher.

There is Christopher Plummer. A Companion of the Order of Canada and recipient of the Governor General's Performing Arts Award for Lifetime Artistic Achievement, Christopher is one of the most talented and acclaimed performers of the stage and screen. I will always remember what he said when he was asked (at a press conference for the Academy Awards in Los Angeles) what the pin on his lapel signified. Christopher replied that he was delighted to inform everyone that it was for an honour he received—the Order of Canada—and that he wore the pin to remind himself that he must always represent the best of his country when he was abroad. He is a teacher.

There are many more. Upon reflection, I would have been more accurate to have said in my installation address as governor general, "cherish and honour our teachers." We should honour our teachers because casting a light on them enables us to recognize the values that make them special, to see reliable examples to emulate, and to build trust throughout our country. One of the best ways for a country to cast that bright light is through an honours system. When I became governor general, I became acquainted very quickly with Canada's. In our country, we are fortunate and perhaps a bit wise to have divided head of state and head of government into the two separate mechanisms. The prime minister and cabinet form the efficient government to carry out the daily business of government. The governor general functions as the dignified government to reflect the fundamental values and protect the Constitution of the country. Canada's honours system is largely lodged within the dignified Crown. This placement is important because it helps ensure that recognition through honours is founded on cherished values and not on wealth, class, or proximity to power.

There are now some seventy different orders for Canada's honours system—all of which are administered by the governor general. Of the seventy, several are honours sanctioned by Her Majesty. Many more are honours, commendations, and certificates of recognition that flow from the governor general's office. This national honours system is replicated and supported in the provinces and territories through the offices of the lieutenant governors and commissioners. It is further bolstered in many municipal governments through mayors, reeves, and regional chairs. Recognition of excellence, achievement, and other values is also present through chambers of commerce, trade and professional associations, and institutions of learning and research. All these systems cast light on many values we should emulate by honouring the people who embody and express these values.

Creating such systems takes work. Canada's honours system is almost as old as the country. The first governor general's honour was established shortly after Confederation. In 1873, Lord Dufferin—the country's third governor general—created the Governor General's Academic Medals for high school and post-secondary school students. This honour continues to this day, with individual medals and letters of congratulations awarded each year to students with the highest academic standing in each of Canada's high schools, university undergraduate programs, and university graduate programs. Since Lord Dufferin's time, honours have grown steadily in number to encompass values such as bravery, innovation, athleticism, professional excellence, scientific success, and artistic achievement.

The best-known honour is the Order of Canada, whose origin is part of the country's evolution from British colony to independent democracy. Until 1919, Canada bestowed titles on its citizens through the British Crown. These titles were largely controlled through the office of the British prime minister and officials at Buckingham Palace. This practice ceased in 1919 with the adoption of the Nickle Resolution by the House of Commons.

It was not until 1967—and the 100th anniversary of Confederation—that our country put in place a made-in-Canada system to honour its most deserving citizens. The reason for the delay is fairly straightforward: as citizens of a largely egalitarian society, Canadians were determined not to replicate the class system of Great Britain. More specifically, the Nickle Resolution was one instance of several in the country's first century in which Canada slowly asserted its independence from Britain. Other milestones on this path are the signing as an independent nation of the 1919 Treaty of Versailles, which put an end formally to the First World War; passage of the Statute of Westminster in 1931, which gave Canada independence in foreign affairs; and abolition of final judicial appeals to the Judicial Committee of the Privy Council of the United Kingdom in 1949.

In 1967, Canada continued this journey when Parliament created the Order of Canada. Much of the credit for the achievement goes to Vincent Massey, our first Canadian-born governor general, who during his tenure, from 1952 to 1959, and after worked to create the honour. Credit also goes to Lester Pearson, the prime minister in 1967 who completed the task. More than most, these two men recognized the enduring worth of trust in Canada and sought to increase trust by honouring people who embody and express the values all Canadians cherish.

The Order of Canada, whose motto is *Desiderantes meliorem patria*, or "They desire a better country," is divided into three levels of recognition: member (for distinction largely at the local level), officer (for distinction that is more national in scope), and companion (for distinction that is national but usually extends beyond Canada's borders). The Chancellery of Honours, which is a self-standing office of a small number of professionals within the Office of the Governor General, administers the Order of Canada. The Chancellery seeks nominations from the public and from various institutions and associations that pursue and recognize excellence. From these nominations, expert opinions are sought from trusted individuals across the country. Then twice a year, the Chancellery presents its recommendations, along with a list of all people considered, to an advisory committee of a dozen or so people.

The governor general appoints members of the committee and the chief justice of the Supreme Court of Canada chairs it. It has been this way since the Order of Canada's inception in 1967. The committee recommends to the governor general the individuals who shall receive the Order of Canada, with the governor general retaining final authority over the decision. On January 1 and July 1 each year, lists of honourees are published. Some months following publication of a list, each honouree is invested in the Order of Canada at a ceremony at Rideau Hall. Honourees are encouraged to wear the distinctive snowflake pin on their lapels or collars to reflect the values of the honour—service, achievement, and contribution to Canada and humanity.

Again, this recognition reflects a deliberate decision made by Canadians to honour people who embody and express the values all Canadians cherish and, in doing so, cast light on reliable examples to emulate. In fact, the Order of Canada is recognized around the world for its respect of the merit principle and the nonpolitical nature of its choices.

While the Chancellery of Honours regularly evaluates representation of the Order of Canada to ensure balance across the country, a major review of the honours system was conducted during my tenure as governor general. The Prime Minister's Office carried out the review since the prime minister is responsible for the overall policy of the Order of Canada, whereas the Office of the Governor General is charged with the independent administration of the policy. As a consequence of the review, we made some changes in this administration. One major change was to increase the number of people invested in the Order of Canada each year to reflect the increase in the country's population. Another big change was to provide more funds to carry out activities to increase awareness of the honours system among Canadians and to seek nominations more proactively. A third change was to enhance several existing honours and create new ones:

- We helped Arnold Witzig and Sima Sharifi develop the Arctic Inspiration Prize, which supports innovative initiatives in the North.
- We expanded the Meritorious Service Decorations, which recognize Canadians for exceptional deeds that bring honour to our country.
- We elevated the Caring Canadian Award to the Sovereign's Medal for Volunteerism and went from awarding several dozen of them each year to more than a thousand annually.
- We increased the number of Polar Medals awarded from one per year to a maximum of fifty. These medals are given

to those who contribute to improving the quality of life in
the North.

- And we created certificates of commendation for the more   189
  than three thousand Canadian university students who are   —
  named academic all-Canadians. These are students who
  represent their schools in a sport and also achieve standing
  on their respective dean's honour lists for academic
  achievement.

We also took steps to give greater prominence to honours outside
the purview of the Office of the Governor General. For instance,
we used the convening power of the Office of the Governor
General to hold annual ceremonies at Rideau Hall to confer
prizes on behalf of the Royal Society of Canada, Canada Council
for the Arts, Social Sciences and Humanities Research Council,
Natural Sciences and Engineering Research Council, Canadian
Institutes of Health Research, and Killam Trust.

In addition, we created a committee on global excellence to
encourage Canadian institutions to nominate our country's most
distinguished researchers and scholars for international prizes.
And we created the Rideau Hall Foundation to amplify and
extend the work of the Office of the Governor General. Through
the Rideau Hall Foundation, we hope to make our honours systems much better known and, in doing so, promote a wider and
better understanding of the values embodied and exemplified by
the honourees.

I outline in some detail here the history of Canada's honours
system and the recent work we carried out in this country to

strengthen and expand this system for a simple reason: honours are the best route a country can take to cast a light on the values

it wishes to promote, to illuminate reliable examples for people to emulate, and to build trust throughout a country. An honour's system brings these values alive.

So let me offer an even more succinct instruction: if you remember only three words of the many I write in this book, remember these: honour our teachers.

19

Be a knowledge diplomat

Sharing knowledge across academic disciplines, cultural barriers, and political borders is the surest way to promote peace, spread prosperity, and build trust among all the people of the world.

The diplomacy of knowledge is my name for the willingness and ability to work across disciplinary boundaries, cultural barriers, and international borders to uncover, share, and refine knowledge. Thomas Jefferson's brilliant metaphor of a burning candle remains the clearest way to illustrate the concept of the diplomacy of knowledge and its incredible power. The candle aflame represents not only enlightenment but also the sharing of knowledge from one person to another. When I light my candle from the flame of yours, your light is not diminished. Just the opposite. The light from both our candles shines even brighter on all around us. Physicists call this light candlepower. An apt term, for there is no power stronger than that of knowledge shared widely.

Why should we practise the diplomacy of knowledge? Why should we be knowledge diplomats? For several very good reasons.

First, when we approach a question from several different angles, we gain a much better sense of its true nature and therefore the best answer. I compare this method to the process of triangulation that surveyors carry out. A surveyor uses instruments such as a level, transit, and theodolite to determine the distances and relative positions of unknown points based on known coordinates.

Second, we must be knowledge diplomats because the biggest challenges we face as individual nations are either global in origin or in scale—ensuring people can access adequate supplies of food and fresh water, reducing or at least mitigating the harmful effects of climate change, and uncovering reliable sources of renewable energy so that we can fuel our industries, communities, and lives. In fact, the future health and wealth of nations will become increasingly defined by how well we develop and advance knowledge. Knowledge—as opposed to military might or gross domestic product—will be the future's currency of success.

Third, we must be knowledge diplomats because it is the surest way to build trust among all the people of the world; when worldwide trust grows stronger, the life of the world has a better chance to become more peaceful.

A wonderful truth about the diplomacy of knowledge is that all people can practise it. Whether we are young or old, students or professionals, each of us has something worthwhile to share based on our particular education and experience. Canadians are excellent knowledge diplomats. We believe deeply in the intrinsic value of learning from one another and sharing knowledge widely—a belief that dates back at least to the first encounters between the country's Indigenous people and European settlers. We have made high-quality public education widely accessible, which has made it possible for generations of Canadians to overcome barriers of racism, poverty, and class and move closer to achieving their true potential. And we encourage new Canadians from countries and cultures around the world to retain and celebrate those aspects of their heritages that do not conflict with the time-honoured values that have made our country such a success. This balanced approach enriches our country by adding the best that others bring—an example of the diplomacy of knowledge at home.

These beliefs and practices—exercised continually—have made Canada a trusted country in the eyes of the world. According to a June 2017 Ipsos poll, respondents put Canada at the top of the list of countries and international organizations (such as the World Bank, International Monetary Fund, and European Union) that have a positive influence on world affairs today. This trust is proving to be resilient, holding steady at the same level measured by Ipsos in 2016. What makes this result even more impressive is that while Canada's score remains steady, those of our country's G7 counterparts—Germany, France, the United Kingdom, and the United States—dropped substantially. In light of these results, the task for Canadians is obvious: to increase their practice of the diplomacy of knowledge, to be knowledge diplomats more than ever.

For seven years, I was privileged to serve in a position in our country that is founded on the practice of the diplomacy of knowledge. Yes, Canada's governor general is the representative of the Crown in Canada and the country's commander in chief of the armed forces. Yet the duty that the governor general performs most often is that of knowledge diplomat—at home but especially abroad. We made fifty-six different country visits during my time as governor general. Our delegations were typically made up of as many as several dozen people: a minister of the Crown; three members of Parliament, each representing one of the major parties; and ten to twenty representatives from trade, cultural, educational, and nongovernmental associations. During these visits, we would all carry out the soft power of the diplomacy of knowledge. (Soft power is a term coined by Harvard University professor Joseph Nye to describe the shaping of preferences of others through appeal and attraction rather than coercion and force.) We would meet a variety of people, exchange with them our respective concerns and ambitions, and identify ways we could work together to share the knowledge necessary to address these concerns and realize these ambitions.

On the airplane returning home from each foreign visit, I always composed a reporting letter to the prime minister. I started by thanking him for asking me to undertake the mission. The governor general travels only at the request of the prime minister. Then I reported on the objectives of the mission and how they were satisfied. I also shared some personal observations about the meetings I had held with the head of state, head of government, and other people in the country we had just visited.

Through these visits, I became a great believer in soft power and the importance of people-to-people relationships, especially when these relationships revolved around the themes of educa- tion, innovation, investment, and trade.

I could relate dozens of examples of the diplomacy of knowledge at work. Let me mention just three. The first comes from Qatar. On my first official visit to this small country on the Arabian Peninsula, I spent several hours with the Sheika, who is the wife of the Qatari Emir, or ruler. She chairs the Qatar Educational Foundation, whose chief executive officer is a distinguished, intelligent, and creative Egyptian. During our discussion, the Sheika outlined her efforts to use the Qatar Educational Foundation to lead an Islamic renaissance that would seek to recapture the flourishing of Islamic civilization that took place from the eighth to the fourteenth century, and build it on modern technology and twenty-first-century knowledge. She indicated that her effort would emphasize primary, secondary, and tertiary education and research relationships between Islam and the Western world.

I was deeply taken by her ambition, and afterward I wrote a long memo to her, in which I shared with her many questions, suggestions, and recommendations based on my knowledge and experience as an educator. For her part, she was intrigued by my personal story—a Canadian from a modest background who left my country at age eighteen to study in the United States and then the United Kingdom. She was particularly interested in the fact that my first university was Harvard, which is some 350 years old, and my second was the University of Cambridge, which is some 800 years old, dating back to the Islamic Golden Age.

She questioned me at length about my life at these two universities, and their world influence, and drew me out on my observations and reflections from these experiences.

One such observation was how rapidly the settler community in the United States put education first. The Puritans, who arrived in Massachusetts Bay in 1620, established Harvard in 1635 to educate the community's ministers. In 1647, the Puritans founded the Massachusetts Bay Colony public schools to ensure that every girl and boy could learn to read and write and do arithmetic. They especially wanted to make sure every child could read the Bible—similar to the motivation of John Wesley in Scotland a century or so later when he established free public schools in Scotland for boys and girls, and ushered in the Scottish enlightenment. The actions of the Massachusetts Bay Colony spurred an American enlightenment.

Several years later, I was in London, England, for an international conference and had a bilateral meeting with the Sheika. This time, among other items for discussion, I had a specific mission: to encourage Qatar to cease its efforts to relocate the International Civil Aviation Authority and the International Air Transport Association to Qatar from their headquarters in Montreal. These two United Nations–sponsored organizations had been set up shortly after the Second World War and established in Montreal as a consequence of the vital role Canada played in aviation during the war. I laid out the case for maintaining these organizations in Montreal, calling on their impressive fifty-plus years of history and achievement. I also referred to the fact that the McGill University faculty of law was the first in the world to establish an international air and space law institute and that I had lectured there occasionally during my time as principal of McGill University. I emphasized that the contribution that the institute had made to the rule of law and to conflict resolution in air and later space—new frontiers—was unparalleled. Like the settlers of the Massachusetts Bay Colony, the institute was a groundbreaker in creating a peace-promoting legal framework for the next frontier—outer space.

The Sheika listened to my presentation and showed surprise. It seemed clear to me that she was not aware of the ambitions of her compatriots and had not been briefed on the matter in advance. A few days later, we learned from our ambassador in Qatar that the Qatari initiative had ceased. I cannot be certain of a cause-and-effect relationship between my discussion with the Sheika and the Qatari's subsequent decision, but my belief in the importance of the diplomacy of knowledge suggests there was one.

Another noteworthy instance of the diplomacy of knowledge took place in Brazil in 2013. During the official visit, I met with President Dilma Rousseff. Apart from some general topics, we had identified two quite specific matters to discuss. The first was the Canada–Brazil Council of CEOs, which was set up by the president's predecessor to parallel a similar organization set up with the United States. One year after the creation of the council, the Canadian chair and members had all long been named and had pressed for meetings with their Brazilian counterparts for some months without success.

When I raised the matter with President Rousseff, she looked quite surprised and then broke into Portuguese, speaking for about five minutes with the three Brazilian ministers who were with her. The temperature of the meeting rose rapidly. She then returned to English, apologized to me for this intervention, and explained that she had told her ministers to attach the greatest importance to this council, and that she wanted immediate action on it. She said that when her predecessor created the Brazil–U.S. council, he appointed the most important person he could find to head it up—herself.

Later in the conversation with the president, we discussed an ambitious program she had established to give 75,000 young Brazilians full scholarships to study abroad. Canada was eager to participate in this exchange, but we learned that, in the first round of scholarships, 20,000 were to go to the United States and the rest were divided among the United Kingdom, France, Germany, and Italy. We in Canada had expected to be included in the first round. We were not.

As part of this mission to Brazil, I was leading a delegation of thirty Canadian university and college presidents who were attending the second edition of the Canada–Brazil Higher Education Forum. Canada had created the forum and had hosted its first meeting two years earlier in Calgary. When I explained that Canada was bypassed in the first round of destinations for Brazilian students, the president again broke into Portuguese to discuss this matter with the ministers. Again, the temperature rose. This time higher.

She then told me that Canada not only would be included in the first round of destinations for students but also would be given priority. She went on to say why she felt it so important for young Brazilians to study in Canada. She cited one by one the quality of our education system, the safety of our cities, our open multicultural society, our comparative low cost of living and education fees, and the fact that Canada would attend to the cultural and social aspects of the exchange, as well as the academic aspects, including working and research internships for the students. She then said something that really hit home with me: "Most of all," she said, "I want young Brazilians to study in Canada because your young people are such excellent role models. They are idealistic, hard working, and civil and have good values." The good news is Canada now has as many of these scholars as the United States, and thanks to the excellent welcoming and educational programs of Canada's universities and colleges, the exchange has been a great success.

The final example involves China. We made two official visits to China during my tenure as governor general. The second was in July 2017, during which we signed three memoranda of agreement. The first memorandum was on behalf of the Canadian Olympic Committee to become a partner in helping China undertake the 2022 Winter Olympics. The second memorandum was on behalf of Hockey Canada to establish community networks across the country to promote hockey and other winter sports. The third memorandum was on behalf of a Canadian consortium that will build ice rinks and other winter sports infrastructure throughout China. During the signing ceremonies, there was frequent reference to President Xi's determination that 300 million Chinese would participate in winter sports in time for the 2022 games. In addition to these memoranda, Canada's ambition is to double the number of Chinese tourists coming to Canada in the next four years. Many of them will come to Canada for winter sports, and many young Canadians will go to China to coach and participate in winter sports.

As I thought about the bridge that sports could provide between Canada and China, my mind travelled back in history to the early 1970s when U.S. president Richard Nixon and secretary of state Henry Kissinger opened the door to China through what was called Ping-Pong diplomacy. The Chinese were world class in table tennis and eager to display their prowess. The Americans used that sport and healthy China–U.S. competition to put the previous frosty relations with China into a much more positive state. I hope that we can follow that precedent through winter sports and a successful China 2022 Winter Olympics. I have continued to work on that ambition, including the trade opportunities, since finishing my tenure as governor general.

A further story from this last Chinese visit will always remain etched in my memory. On the final day of the visit, Carla Qualtrough, who was minister of sport and persons with disabilities at the time, and I met with representatives of a nongovernmental organization called SOS. It is a group that promotes the rights of persons with disabilities, who have long been neglected in China. SOS is supported by the Canadian embassy in China, which used some modest discretionary funds to help create or reinforce volunteer organizations. This area is one in which Canada has some expertise. The representatives with whom we met had a particular focus on blindness. They themselves were blind. They explained that the Canadian embassy had provided the funds and expertise to train volunteers to assist blind people throughout China.

One of the special interventions was to arrange for the translation and then the mentoring of instructors to ensure that all the entrance examinations to Chinese universities for the first time ever could be done in Braille. As a consequence, the first blind Chinese student was admitted to a Chinese university in 2015. Remember, China has been conducting examinations for young men—now young men and women—to enter the public service as mandarins for almost two thousand years. Only a few moments into this conversation, Carla and I had tears running down our cheeks. Carla explained to the group that even though she was legally blind, she has gone to university and then law school, that she had participated in the Paralympic Games and won medals as a swimmer, and that she had become a minister of the Crown. In my case, my mother became blind by the age of forty-five and, therefore, opportunities for blind people and more generally disabled people have long had a very special place in my heart. Jefferson's candle was burning brightly.

All these examples show the diplomacy of knowledge at work. They show the mutual advantages that come when Canadians share knowledge across academic disciplines, cultural barriers, and political borders. They show how the diplomacy of knowledge is a powerful human force in taking on and solving big challenges. They show how each of us can be knowledge diplomats because each of us has wisdom and experiences worth sharing. And sharing our individual flames of enlightenment is the surest way to make Canada a more trusted country and build trust among all the people of the world.

20

Start now

Each of us can begin strengthening trust and,
with our actions, make our country better.

As governor general of Canada for seven years, I led dozens of delegations of Canadians on fifty-six missions to thirty-five countries on every continent except Antarctica. And I would have been thrilled to go even there if either Prime Minister Harper or Prime Minister Trudeau had asked me! During these official visits, I met kings and queens, popes and princes, presidents and prime ministers. We talked about many significant subjects: innovation, education, immigration, health care, technology, philanthropy, volunteerism, families, children, diversity, inclusion, and justice. I also spoke with many Canadians who were working and studying abroad, and I encouraged countless young citizens in the countries I visited to come to Canada to work and study. Above all, I tried to spread messages of hope, optimism, and collaboration on behalf of my country and then bring home and share with Canadians what I heard, saw, and learned from other places.

What I learned most from these visits is that no problem is solved, no challenge tackled, no opportunity seized without trust among nations, trust between people and the institutions that are meant to serve and represent them, and above all trust among people. If we are to make Canada the smart and caring country we want it to be, and if we are to make a meaningful contribution in creating a smarter and more caring world, we as Canadians—individually and together—must make ourselves more worthy of trust and sharpen our judgement when placing our trust in other people, businesses, organizations, and institutions.

My experiences and the lessons that flowed from them also got me thinking more critically than ever before about the state of trust in countries throughout the world and in Canada. What I found was both discouraging and encouraging.

First, the discouraging: as I mentioned in the introduction, Edelman, the global public relations company that has been surveying trust for two decades, revealed in its 2017 Trust Barometer that trust is in crisis around the world. People's trust in four vital institutions—business, government, nongovernment organizations, and media—has dropped broadly and dramatically. Edelman concluded:

With the fall of trust, the majority of respondents now lack full belief that the overall system is working for them. In this climate, people's societal and economic concerns, including globalization, the pace of innovation and eroding social values, turn into fears, spurring the rise of populist actions now playing out in several Western-style democracies.

The 2017 results were particularly bad for Canada. For the first time in the many years that Edelman has been researching its Trust Barometer, Canada went from being in the "neutral" category and slipped down into the many "distruster" nations. The following year's results were not much better. The 2018 Edelman Trust Barometer revealed what the company calls "a world of seemingly stagnant distrust." According to the Edelman findings, people's trust in business, government, nongovernment organizations, and media is largely unchanged from 2017, with 20 of 28 countries surveyed sitting in distruster territory. The most notable difference from 2017 to 2018 is that the media is the least-trusted institution globally. Edelman concludes that "the demise of confidence in the Fourth Estate is driven primarily by a significant drop in trust in platforms, notably search engines and social media."

Canada typified the stagnant results. Our country was among the distruster nations for the second straight year. Yet, for the first time in the history of the Edelman study, global companies headquartered in Canada are the most trusted in the world. This finding echoes one from research done by Ipsos: respondents place Canada atop a list of countries and international organizations that have a positive influence on world affairs. So while levels of trust in most countries around the world have decreased, these same people are placing their trust in Canada more and more. This happy trend, as I point out in a previous chapter, speaks to our success as knowledge diplomats. This advantage is one that Canadian businesses and executives should use to export trust, and not just goods and services, worldwide. It is also a challenge that Canadians should rise to: let us make decisions and take actions that make ourselves worthy of the continuing trust of the world. If, as the Indigo Books slogan has it, the world needs more Canada, then let us give the world our very best.

Proof Inc., a Canadian communications company, also researches trust; the company centres its study on Canada. As the organization states, it "takes a distinctly Canadian approach to measuring and tracking Canadians' trust in leaders, industries and information sources, and uncovers themes, trends and perspectives that tell us who we are." The findings of the Proof CanTrust Index 2017 mirror those of the Edelman study—with one notable exception. This is the encouraging part. Proof did a deep dive into the trust of new Canadians and found that these citizens kept Canadians overall from being distrusters. As its report states: "In the wake of a rise in protectionism and distrust in immigrants in some countries … we see a culture where New Canadians are driving the optimism of our country, perhaps pointing in turn to a hopeful future for companies and governments seeking to grow consumer trust." The title of the 2017 Proof report reflects this differentiator clearly and cleverly: "Trust Canada to Be Different."

Again this year, results of the Proof CanTrust Index survey mirror those of the most recent Edelman study: Canadians are straddling the 50 per cent mark. Half of us are trusting and half are not. The Proof Inc. survey also reflects the Edelman findings in another notable respect: business sectors are regaining the trust of Canadians. We appear to be looking to business leaders and brands to fill the void in trust being left by the country's public institutions and media. Most notable to me, however, is that Proof finds that new Canadians continue to be more trusting than their fellow citizens. Results show that citizens who have lived in Canada for fewer than fifteen years are more trusting than those born in this country and who were not born in Canada but who have lived here for more than fifteen years.

The conclusion I draw from the Proof CanTrust indices is unmistakable: Canadians must make sure the country's newest citizens not only are represented in its businesses, organizations, and institutions but also are genuinely included in the decisions and actions these groups take. The findings from the important research carried out by Edelman and Proof—especially the significant influence that new Canadians have on trust—also led my thinking on how the decline of trust in our country and worldwide was not going to be reversed solely through the actions and admonitions of kings and queens, presidents and prime ministers—or even governors general. Nor was it going to be reversed merely by a national campaign organized and directed by some central authority—no matter how trusted and influential that authority might be. And it certainly was not going to be reversed by time, patience, or hope. I think that if new

208
—

Canadians—the people who are seemingly most in need of special care, support, and protection as they adjust to life in this country—are doing the most to bolster trust in Canada, then surely each and every Canadian has the ability within them to reverse the decline in trust in our country. Taking our cue from our country's newest citizens, we all could and should start at home; we could and should start small; and most of all we could and should start now.

The more I thought about this approach, the more I realized how effective it could be—because I had seen it being done time and time again. For seven years as governor general, I travelled to hundreds of neighbourhoods, towns, and cities in every part of this huge country—north, south, east, west, and all points on the compass in between. Truth be told, my favourite part of the job was the meetings I had with mayors, reeves, councillors, and First Nations chiefs right across Canada—from Windsor to Alert, from Vancouver Island to the Rock of Newfoundland. In listening to these local leaders, I learned how Canadians were taking the actions necessary to build trust at home right now.

In Calgary, I learned from Mayor Naheed Nenshi how he heeded the advice of the city's civic engagement committee, which convinced him to forgo a grand municipal celebration of Canada's 150th birthday and instead to centre the city's efforts on encouraging each citizen of Calgary to uncover and express three of their own ways to make the city better. Known as "3 Things for Calgary," the campaign caught on and spread across the country, becoming "3 Things for Canada" and inspiring people from all towns, cities, and regions to get more involved in the life of their communities in ways that were meaningful to them. Mayor Nenshi, in particular, showed how trust is built by listening first, by knowing that there is more than one right way, and by recog- 209 nizing that his success is dependent on those around him. —

In Rimouski, I learned from Mayor Éric Forest how the city went about naming its major junior hockey team. Mayor Forest said that city leaders believed the team should not only showcase athletic skill and competitiveness but also reflect Rimouski's desire to be renowned as an international centre for oceanic research and discovery. After all, the city was home to four distinguished organizations of marine study: the Institut des sciences de la mer, the Centre de recherche sur les biotechnologies marines, the Centre interdisciplinaire de développement en cartographie des océans, and the St. Lawrence Global Observatory. To display the city's passion for the world's oceans and use that display to attract professionals who share this enthusiasm, Rimouski named its team Océanic. The city's decision is a down-home example of being true to one's self—of getting a fix on what it values and letting decisions flow from that.

In Churchill, I learned from Mayor Mike Spence how the town had been hit hard economically by the shutdown of the rail line from Winnipeg. For generations, this steel spur had enabled Churchill to remain an important transit point in the shipment of grain from the Prairies to markets in Eastern Canada and across the Atlantic. At first, I was surprised to learn from Mayor Spence that one of the main steps the town was taking to respond to this commercial hardship was placing a greater emphasis on reconciliation with First Nations, Métis, and Inuit people in the town and its surrounding area. The mayor then explained the reason behind this renewed emphasis and my surprise vanished. If Churchill were to find solutions to overcome this adversity, Mayor Spence said, the town needed to involve absolutely all its people in the effort. Everyone needed to be included—not only to focus more minds on solving the problem, but more so because the only viable solution was one that would work for all people. Churchill's action is an illustration of informing everyone of the plan—of trusting citizens to extend to its fullest their collective ability to understand the complexities of a problem and take action to solve it. The city's action also reflects its awareness of the value of giving a meaningful opportunity to contribute to civic decisions—of inviting others to dance, not just inviting them to the dance.

In the Okanagan Valley, I learned from Clarence Louie, chief of the Osoyoos Indian Band, his recipe for building a thriving community. It starts with forging productive relations with neighbouring communities. The Osoyoos Nation has built a strong working relationship with wineries in nearby communities. Chief Louie told me how an owner of a neighbouring vineyard traded some valuable land connected to reserve territory for more distant land owned by the Osoyoos Indian Band. Chief Louie then convinced the vineyard owner to share his winemaking expertise with the Osoyoos people, who used that expertise to produce award-winning wines that are served regularly at state banquets and other receptions at Rideau Hall.

Chief Louie also told me how a provincial penitentiary had come to be located on Osoyoos territory. Some years ago, the

British Columbia government placed a call for tenders for land on which to build a medium-security prison. Chief Louie and the Osoyoos prepared and presented what turned out to be the winning bid. The government then placed a call for tenders to build the penitentiary. Again, the Osoyoos prepared and presented a bid, this time through the community's construction company. Yet again, the community was successful. Chief Louie told me that he found no use in going to Ottawa for meetings. Too much talk, too little done, he said. I stay here and help create jobs, he added. We were just about finished our conversation when the chief's phone rang. I encouraged him not to stand on ceremony and to answer it. He excused himself, picked up his phone, and had a brief talk with the caller. He concluded the chat by saying, "Yes, let's get started. Meet me here tomorrow morning. Eight o'clock. Sharp."

I smile even now thinking about Chief Louie's instruction, because his approach is a most vivid and literal illustration of the admonition "Start now. Sharp." He and his community are not waiting for others to arrive on the Osoyoos's doorstep with opportunities and solutions. He and his people take the initiative and create their own. In doing so, they have built a community and public institutions within it that are trusted by its members and trusted by institutions and individuals throughout the province.

I could supply dozens of additional instances of how Canadians have taken action to restore and strengthen trust close to home. These examples prove that communities, cities, and countries in which people trust each other have the cohesion to solve problems, the commitment to seize opportunities, and the resilience to survive setbacks. On the flip side, communities, cities, and countries that lack trust are often unwilling to admit they have problems, let alone have the cohesion necessary to unite in tackling them; they are unable to seize opportunities because they lack any shared commitment about which goals to strive toward, let alone which direction to take to get there; they are unable to weather misfortune, let alone bounce back from it.

Our mission as Canadians then must be to rebuild and continually strengthen trust in our country so that we can overcome our most enduring problems, seize our every opportunity, reverse all our setbacks, and make ourselves worthy of trust in the eyes of the world. Education will play a prominent role in the rebuilding. Learning and trust are inseparable. Thanks to Edelman and Proof, the learning is underway and will continue. I urge both organizations to carry on their excellent work in tracking the state of trust in Canada and the world. Their surveys, findings, and reports supply us with the ongoing results we need to measure any progress we make in rebuilding trust and to identify areas of most concern.

These pages also present several suggestions to use education to rebuild trust. For instance, we should make it possible for many more young people to be exposed to the world; we should change how we teach, so that young people can improve their ability to judge and heighten their awareness of trust; and we all should become much more discerning consumers and sharers of news and information.

Of course, this book is an invitation to learn about twenty ways in which we can take action to build trust. They stem from my experiences and what these experiences have taught me about trust. Start taking that necessary action. Start close to home—using these actions in the places where you believe they can have the most immediate influence. Start small—with one or two actions that make the most sense to you. Start now—begin making yourself more worthy of trust and sharpening your judgement when placing trust in others.

If you doubt your ability to increase trust to a meaningful degree, let me assure you that individual actions produce chemical changes in a society, rather than mere arithmetical increases. Many years ago, Mother Teresa, the famed nun who founded the Missionaries of Charity, made her first visit to Canada to share with Canadians the story of her work to help the sick and destitute of Calcutta. An editorial in a major Canadian newspaper lauded her intentions but lamented the ultimate futility of her efforts. What good came from helping hundreds, the editorialist concluded, when millions were in need?

I knew in my heart that this view was wrong, but I could not quite figure out why. The resolution to my quandary came from an unlikely source: the magician at a child's birthday party, who slyly transformed a glass of water into "wine" with the help of a drop of red food colouring. I realized then that the newspaper editorial had approached Mother Teresa's work from the perspective of arithmetic, when her efforts were more properly seen as a form of chemistry. Her seemingly small changes catalyzed others to make changes of their own. She was altering the very nature of the glass of water, not adding to or subtracting from it.

I urge you to heed this lesson in chemistry. Just as a drop of food colouring changes water from clear to coloured, so too can each of us take meaningful action now to make ourselves more worthy of trust, and to restore trust in the communities in which we live, the businesses and organizations in which we work, and the public institutions in which we serve. By heeding this lesson and acting in the twenty ways I have identified, each of us can carry out our foremost duty as citizens of this country—we can build a better Canada.

Acknowledgements

Leadership is recognizing your total dependence on the people around you. As this book made its journey from conception to execution to publication, I was profoundly and repeatedly aware of just how accurate this observation is.

I depended, as I have in all important ventures in my life, on the love, encouragement, and wisdom of Sharon, my wife, and our five daughters—Deborah, Alexandra, Sharon, Jenifer, and Sam.

I depended on the expertise and generosity of Lisa Kimmel of Edelman Canada and Bruce MacLellan of Proof Inc.—two professionals whose organizations study trust closely and have made their findings and analysis available to me and to all Canadians.

I depended on the kindness and intelligence of a group of people who read this book in manuscript and made many valuable suggestions to improve it. They are Jennifer Brennan, Michael Caesar, Lois Claxton, Annabelle Cloutier, Richard

T R U S T

Cruess, Sylvia Cruess, Chad Gaffield, Roberta Jamieson, the Right Honourable Beverley McLachlin, James Mitchell, and Stephen Wallace. My special thanks go to former chief justice McLachlin for contributing the wise and generous words that begin this book.

218
—

I depended on the constant support and counsel of my col-leagues at the Rideau Hall Foundation. My special thanks go to our former president and CEO Scott Haldane, our new presi-dent and CEO Teresa Marques, Barbara Gibbon, and especially Kelly-Ann Benoit.

I depended on the skilled team of publishing professionals at Signal/McClelland & Stewart. My special thanks go to Kimberlee Hesas, Wendy Thomas, Aeman Ansari, Five Seventeen, and espe-cially publisher Doug Pepper for his constant encouragement and enthusiasm.

And I depended on Brian Hanington and John Phillips of Stiff Inc. This is our third major shared writing project. I relied on them to help conceive, research, and then produce this book. Quite simply, it was trust exceedingly well placed and rewarded.

ABOUT THE AUTHOR

David Johnston is a Canadian citizen, thinker, advocate, and leader. A graduate of Harvard, Cambridge, and Queen's universities, he served recently as one of Canada's most respected and beloved governors general. Before that, he was president of the University of Waterloo, principal of McGill University, and dean of law at Western University. Today, he is chair of the Rideau Hall Foundation (the charitable organization he helped found in 2012) and advisor at Deloitte and at Fairfax Financial Holdings. David is a Companion of the Order of Canada, and he holds honorary doctorates from thirty-six universities. He also is author or co-author of more than thirty books and was the first governor general of Canada to publish a book of nonfiction while in office. He will direct all royalties he receives from the sale of *Trust* (as was the case with his three most recent books: *The Idea of Canada*, *Ingenious*, and *Innovation Nation*) to the Rideau Hall Foundation to support its important work serving Canadians through a range of initiatives linked to leadership, learning, giving, and innovation. Born in Sudbury, Ontario, raised in Sault Ste. Marie, Ontario, and now living near Ottawa, Ontario, David is married to Sharon Johnston; they have five daughters and fourteen grandchildren.

A NOTE ABOUT THE TYPE

Trust is set in Adobe Caslon, a digitized typeface based on the original 1734 designs of William Caslon. Caslon is generally regarded as the first British typefounder of consequence and his fonts are considered, then as now, to be among the world's most "user-friendly" text faces.